SUN VALLEY

CELEBRITIES & LOCAL HEROES

COOKBOOK, SECOND EDITION

Compiled & Edited by Jennifer R. Diehl
for The Advocates for Survivors of
Domestic Violence and Sexual Assault

a place
to go...

The Advocates

helping people build safe lives

Sun Valley Celebrities & Local Heroes Cookbook, Second Edition

Project Manager: Jennifer R. Diehl
Compiled & Edited: Jennifer R. Diehl
Cover & interior artwork: Will Caldwell
Layout & Design: Mountain Media, Erika DiCello
Proofreading: Premi Pearson

Cover Art: Prints of this painting are available to purchase,
with partial proceeds to benefit The Advocates.
To order, please call Will Caldwell at 208.726.9059.

All proceeds from the sale of this cookbook directly benefit
The Advocates for use in aiding victims of domestic violence.
For additional copies, dealer inquiries, or group gifts, please contact:

The Advocates for Survivors of Domestic Violence & Sexual Assault

Post Office Box 3216
Hailey, Idaho 83333
tel 208.788.4191
fax 208.788.4194

Published by The Advocates for Survivors of Domestic Violence & Sexual Assault

© 2001 The Advocates for Survivors of Domestic Violence & Sexual Assault
ISBN 0-9713157-0-1
Library of Congress Control Number: 2001135190
First Printing
Printed in China

About Will Caldwell. . .

Will Caldwell provided the lovely picturesque Sun Valley scenic paintings that grace this cookbook's cover and section pages. Will Caldwell lives with his family on the back side of Baldy and has shown his art locally and nationally since 1975. The search for painting subjects has led him to five continents and his work has been shown in a dozen western states. His paintings are in collections as diverse as the National Archives of Kenya, George Lucas in Hollywood and the Coca Cola Corporate Museum in Florida. Currently, Will's paintings are on exhibit in Telluride, Colorado, at the Sagebrush Gallery in Ketchum and the Sun Valley Art Gallery on the Sun Valley Mall.

The splendor of Sun Valley draws unique individuals who constantly give back to our community, and this cookbook reflects the wonderful diversity of those who live in the Wood River Valley and spend time here. This is just a sampling, for our community is filled with talented, industrious, warm and generous people. Many thanks to all of the recipe contributors, who took the time to sit down and thoughtfully put together the materials we required. I cannot thank you enough for that. Without you, there wouldn't be a cookbook!

I would like to thank The Advocates for the opportunity to work on such a remarkable project. I have met so many amazing people and have had a most rewarding experience compiling this cookbook. Many thanks to Sheila Liermann, who set the stage for this sequel.

Tricia Swartling and her staff at The Advocates' office always stopped what they were doing to help me out, and The Advocates' Board was very generous with their support and feedback. Thanks to you all!

Much gratitude goes to Premi Pearson for her hard work, to Erika DiCello and Diane Moberg for being so enjoyable to work with, and to Express Printing, DMI and P. Chan & Edward for turning production around so quickly.

Will Caldwell once again contributed the artwork that graces this cookbook. Thank you, Will, your generosity is heartfelt.

I would also like to acknowledge and thank the following people for putting me in touch with many of the recipe contributors: Lynn Bailey, Kate Berman, Jennifer Copeland, Jennifer Dies, Kathryn Gardner, Alysia May, Larry Flynn, Molly Goodyear, Anne Kalik, Pamela Sue Martin, Nita Mott, Riley Mott, Ann Neary, Gretchen Palmer, Kim Payes, Sue Rowland, Tricia Swartling, Jeffra Syms, Leigh Walters, Chuck Webb and Susan Winget.

And finally, deepest thanks to my family. Brent, you gave me the encouragement to pull this off! Hunter, your birth gave me the inspiration to start something new. And Mom and Dad, your endless support kept me going.

I couldn't have done this project without my extraordinary team.

Jennifer R. Diehl

The Advocates is the only domestic violence and sexual assault program serving the Wood River Valley and its surrounding counties. The organization is committed to providing victims of domestic violence and sexual assault with the resources needed for safety, empowerment and prevention of further victimization. Our ultimate goal is to end domestic violence and sexual assault in our communities.

Through our dedicated staff and volunteers, we offer a wide variety of effective services ranging from safe transitional shelter and court advocacy to counseling and prevention programs in the schools and community. These programs are run by fourteen paid staff members and more than twenty volunteers. Services are available in Spanish and English, 24 hours a day, free of charge. A Community Advisory Committee and twelve-member Board of Directors representative of the community provide guidance for the organization.

The Advocates assists over 300 women and 100 children annually. In December 1999, we completed construction on and opened our first local domestic violence shelter. The shelter is a wheelchair-accessible, five-bedroom, four-bath house that can accomodate up to 20 individuals. We are happy to report that the shelter is making a difference in the lives of many local families. Each year, more than 40 women and 35 children are provided over 1,500 nights of shelter.

The shelter's annual operating budget is over $300,000. Funding comes from the following sources: local government 5%, federal and state government 30%, private foundations 25%, fund-raising 25%, endowment income 8%, and unsolicited contributions 7%. Fund-raising efforts include one large annual event, two to four smaller events, sales of the *Sun Valley Celebrities and Local Heroes Cookbook, Second Edition* and an annual donation request letter to the community. From the sale of this cookbook over the next four years, we hope to raise over $300,000 to support our shelter.

Thank you to all contributors to the cookbook. We appreciate the time everyone took to give us a recipe and personal information. Thanks also to all of you who have purchased this book. We hope the cookbook further inspires you to help stop domestic violence. If you would like to learn more about the Advocates, become a volunteer or make a financial contribution, please contact us at 208.788.4191.

Enjoy reading and cooking with the celebrities and local heroes that spend time in the Wood River Valley. Bon appétit!

Susan Stanek Winget
President, Board of Directors

Tricia Swartling
Executive Director

APPETIZERS & DRINKS

GUACAMOLE

FROM ROB FRIEDMAN

2 ripe avocados

1 small jalapeño chili, seeded and minced

$1/2$ small onion, minced

3-4 teaspoons fresh lime juice

$1/4$ cup chopped cilantro

$1/4$ cup chopped tomato

Dash of Tabasco sauce

Salt & pepper to taste (use kosher salt)

Mash avocados, then add all other ingredients, blending until smooth.

Robert G. Friedman is Vice Chairman of the Motion Picture Group of Paramount Pictures, where he is responsible for worldwide theatrical marketing and distribution of feature films and Home Entertainment. Among his marketing and distribution accomplishments are *What Women Want, Mission: Impossible-2, Runaway Bride,* and *Titanic*, the highest-grossing film in history and winner of 11 Academy Awards.

When he finds time to relax, Rob enjoys coming to Sun Valley to hike, fish, play golf and ski.

SUSIE'S BEST MICROWAVE POPCORN

FROM SUSIE PATTERSON

My skiing opened up many opportunities for me. My husband, Ned Gillette introduced me to a life of traveling all over the world, writing about and photographing our adventures. Returning home to Sun Valley is the highlight of going away. Of course, skiing will always be in my blood, but it's the unusual beauty that is always changing with the seasons, the eclectic naturalness of the people and the security of our tucked-away little valley that make it home for me, a utopia we should all feel honored to live in.

I hope this recipe is taken in the spirit I intended — for fun! It goes without saying that cooking isn't exactly my forté, but this really is my favorite and best recipe.

1 Bag of Microwave Popcorn

Tabasco Sauce

Remove plastic overwrap, make sure the bag has no holes, tears, or broken seals.

Unfold the bag and place alone in center of microwave oven, directions-side up.

Microwave on high (full power) until bag is expanded and popping slows to 2 seconds between pops. Normal popping time is 1-4 minutes. Do not overcook, as popcorn may scorch. Do not leave microwave unattended while popping corn. Remove bag from oven carefully. (It's hot!)

Open top of bag by pulling diagonally at corners.

To spice it up, shake on Tabasco sauce.

Susie Patterson

Adventure Photojournalist Susie Patterson Gillette grew up skiing on the Sun Valley Ski Team, and was on the US Olympic Alpine Ski Team in 1976 and World Championship Ski Teams in 1976 and 1978. She is a former US National Downhill Champion and US National Slalom Champion, and was the top competitor on the US World Cup Ski Team from 1970 to 1980. Susie was the ABC Sports Color commentator for the 1980 Olympics.

SALSA

FROM DR. MELANI HARKER

2 tablespoons olive oil

1 large onion, chopped

5 cloves garlic, chopped

2 pounds tomatoes, peeling optional

10-15 assorted peppers
(jalepeño, serrano, habanero …)

Sauté the onion and garlic in olive oil until transparent. Blend the tomatoes and peppers in a blender. In a large pot, add all ingredients and bring to a boil, then simmer uncovered for one hour. Salt to taste.

Optional additives after cooking:

$1/3$ cup fresh cilantro, chopped

1 cup cooked corn kernels

1 avocado, mashed

1 can black beans

Melani Harker, M.D., moved to the Wood River Valley with her family in 1999 to practice Obstetrics and Gynecology. She is highly regarded by her patients and is known for her warmth, ease and support when a baby is on the way. When she takes a break from her busy practice, Melani enjoys hiking, trail running, skate skiing and outdoor concerts. Her favorite food is takeout (other than this salsa, of course)!

PIONEER SALSA

FROM THE PIONEER SALOON

This salsa is a traditional delight for those who get to the Pioneer early enough for happy hour!

6 $\frac{1}{2}$ pounds tomatoes, diced

6 $\frac{1}{2}$ pounds tomato sauce

27 ounces diced green chiles

2 $\frac{1}{2}$ ounces Tabasco sauce

2 medium onions, chopped

1 bunch cilantro

1 tablespoon salt

1 tablespoon black pepper

4 tablespoons lemon juice

$\frac{1}{2}$ teaspoon garlic

Mix and chill!

THE PIONEER SALOON

The Pioneer Saloon, originally called the Commercial Club, was built in 1945 and operated as a gambling casino by Otis Hobbs. A few years later, the casino was closed for serving minors. The American Legion then took it over and used it as a meeting hall. Not long after, the building was converted into a dry goods store.

Around 1950, the building was reopened as a gambling casino by Whitey Hirschman, who named it the Pioneer Saloon. Although never legal in Idaho, gambling flourished in Ketchum until 1953, when the law intervened. Whitey operated the Pioneer as a bar and colorful antique store until the spring of 1965.

The present version of the Pioneer Saloon dates from 1972: hence the phrase "Where were you in '72," the theme of the Pioneer's annual Oldies but Goodies celebration held each November. And it's known throughout town that if you haven't been to the Pioneer, you haven't been to Ketchum!

KATHARINE'S CRAB APPETIZER

FROM WENDY JAQUET

2 packages cream cheese

1-2 tablespoons butter

Bottle of chile sauce with seeds

$^1/_2$ jar of dry horseradish

$^1/_2$ pound crab

Mix the cream cheese and butter. Place on a piece of Saran wrap on a pie dish and press the cream cheese mixture into the shape of a pie bottom.

Cool in the refrigerator until hard.

Combine the chili sauce and horseradish.

Invert the cream cheese mixture onto an oversized plate. Cover with crab. Pour the chile mixture on top of the crab, covering the cream cheese. Surround the appetizer with Waverley Crackers.

Wendy and Jim Jaquet moved to Ketchum in 1977 because it was such a good place to raise their two sons, Michael and Brian. Jim was the newly selected City Administrator for Ketchum. Wendy served on a variety of Boards, including the Community Library, the Sun Valley Ski Education Foundation and the Sun Valley Center, while being employed as Director of the Sun Valley-Ketchum Chamber of Commerce. In 1994, Wendy was elected to the Idaho State Legislature as a representative for District 21, which includes the Wood River Valley. In 1998, Wendy was chosen by her caucus to be the Minority Leader for the Idaho House of Representatives.

The Jaquets thought they came for the winter sports, but have grown to love the summers just as much. They especially like to hike the trails right out the front door of their home in Hulen Meadows.

COWBOY SASHIMI

Fresh ahi seared Southwestern-style with sesame-crusted risotto vegetable cakes and a tomatillo Adobo Coulis make for an East-meets-West (and North and South) recipe with lots of fun and flavor!

Ahi

1 pound ahi

1 teaspoon paprika

1 teaspoon dark chili powder

1 teaspoon salt

1 teaspoon black pepper

1 teaspoon coriander, ground

1 teaspoon cumin, ground

1 teaspoon oregano, ground

Risotto Cakes

3 tablespoons olive oil

2 cups risotto rice

2 tablespoons each diced carrot, green pepper, red pepper and onion

2 tablespoons corn, cut

1 tablespoon garlic, minced

3 cups chicken stock

2 cups sesame seeds

Adobo Coulis

8 tomatillos (green Mexican tomatoes)

2 cloves garlic, minced

1 onion, chopped

2 tablespoons fresh cilantro, chopped

1 jalapeño pepper, diced

$\frac{1}{2}$ cup white wine

Chef Paul Dean has been cooking professionally for thirty years, starting as an apprentice in a French bistro at the age of 13. After traveling the world for eight years, he returned to the United States to further his career as Executive Chef for the Ritz Carlton, Hyatt and Hilton.

Paul met his wife, Tana, in Jackson Hole, and they lived briefly in Hawaii; but he never lost his love for the mountains. So Paul and Tana moved to the Wood River Valley after just one spring fishing trip. Knowing this was the place they wanted to live and work, they purchased The Wild Radish restaurant sight unseen! They've never looked back. Chef Paul and Tana are the owners of The Wild Radish, the Coyote Grill and The Borhof Bar.

Ahi: Cut and block ahi; chill. Mix together ahi spices. Cut ahi block into four 4-ounce pieces and roll pieces in spice mixture, covering completely. Heat a sauté pan to high and sear the ahi on each side until it takes on a darkened roasted look, not blackened. Do not use any oil or butter! The pan should be completely dry. Remove ahi and chill again.

Risotto Cakes: Heat a pan to medium-high; add olive oil and risotto rice. Stir constantly until olive oil is absorbed by the rice. Add vegetables and garlic, then lower heat to medium. Sauté for five minutes, then add chicken stock; salt and pepper to taste. Stir every few minutes until rice is al dente like pasta. Spread on a cookie sheet and cool in refrigerator.

Adobo Coulis: Heat a 1-quart sauté pan to medium-high. Sauté garlic, onion and jalapeño pepper for 5 minutes. Add white wine and cilantro. Remove husks and dice tomatillos, but do not remove the seeds. Add to mixture and cook 3 minutes. Chill.

Presentation: Put sesame seeds on flat surface. Cut the risotto cakes with a pastry cutter or a glass. Roll in sesame seeds, covering cakes completely. Place cakes in a warm oven on a flat pan until they are warm, not hot; then place in center of plate. Drizzle Adobo Coulis around plate. Cut ahi sashimi-style, approximately 12 pieces, and arrange around the Risotto Cakes. Serves 6 to 10.

HOUSE-CURED SALMON GRAVLAX & SWEET CORN BLINI

FROM PLĀCE

Though this recipe involves several separate components, the cure requires preparation well in advance, so final prep time is shortened significantly.

Gravlax:

1 pound salmon,
with skin, pin boned

$^3/_4$ cup kosher salt

$^1/_2$ cup granulated sugar

$^1/_3$ cup dark brown sugar, packed

8 juniper berries

Zest of 2 lemons

1 bay leaf

1 star anise

1 teaspoon freshly ground pepper

$^1/_4$ bunch thyme

$^1/_4$ bunch sage

Sweet Corn Blini:

$^1/_2$ cup all-purpose flour

$^1/_2$ cup cornmeal

$1^1/_2$ teaspoons baking powder

$^3/_4$ teaspoon salt

Pinch cayenne

$^1/_2$ cup crème fraîche
(or sour cream)

$1^1/_2$ teaspoons honey

$^1/_4$ cup beer

2 ears "cornmilk"
(see instructions below)

1 egg yolk

1 egg white

plāce

Chefs/owners Steven and Rebecca Ludwig describe their menu at Plāce as seasonal comfort food, artfully prepared to taste good! They believe that the consummate dining experience is most often provided by paying mindful attention to the small things. From organic produce to the perfect bottle of wine; from the amuse-bouche on Grandma's china to casually nuanced service given by charming locals, the details are all in Place!

Gravlax: Combine all seasonings in a food processor for two minutes or until ingredients are fully incorporated. Sprinkle $^1/_3$ of cure mixture on bottom of a container sized to fit fish. Place the salmon onto the cure and cover with remaining mixture. Cover tightly and refrigerate for 4 days. Rinse gravlax under cold water.

Serving note: As an easy alternative to slicing the salmon, gravlax can be diced tartar-style and served loosely plated or shaped in a ring

Sweet Corn Blini: Grate two ears of corn with a box grater to create "milk." Separate the egg; whip whites and reserve. Combine all wet ingredients except egg white.

Sift together all dry ingredients. Fold the wet ingredients into the dry ingredients, then fold in the whipped egg white. Heat 2 tablespoons oil in a heavy skillet over medium heat. Spoon batter into the skillet with a sauce spoon, making "pancakes" or blini. Brown each side until cooked through. Makes approximately 24-30 blini.

Final presentation: Top each blini with salmon gravlax and garnish with lemon crème fraîche and cucumber salad. It's also terrific presented with traditional caviar garnishes such as snipped chives or red onion.

MOCK CHOPPED LIVER

FROM BOB BEATTIE

I'm not the cook in our home, so this recipe comes from my wife, Marci. It's one of my favorite appetizers.
No one will ever guess what you made, but I guarantee they'll love it! Bon Appetit!

15-ounce package of Le Sueur Sweet Peas

$1/2$ cup chopped walnuts

2 hard boiled eggs

1 sweet white onion, chopped

1 slice pumpernickel bread or 4 slices "cocktail" pumper nickel (the loaves are small and come in a long package)

Dash of salt

Sauté onion in butter and oil until softened, not brown.

In a cuisenart, separate each ingredient and chop well. Then add all ingredients and blend until just mixed. Put mixture in a serving crock and add a dash of salt to the top. Serve with crackers.

In the summer of 1954, Bob Beattie first visited Sun Valley to help cut trails on Baldy. It was his summer job between semesters at Middlebury College. During the 1960s, he returned as coach of the US Ski Team, and brought World Cup events and a team event called the American International to Sun Valley.

Bob and Marci continue to visit Sun Valley for the skiing.

Bob Beattie

CALIMARI PICANTE

FROM FELIX'S RESTAURANT

Felix's Calamari Picante has earned rave reviews as both an appetizer and an entrée. Enjoy!

Calamari steaks, cut in strips,
dusted lightly with flour and salt

In a skillet, heat olive oil and flash-fry calamari strips to a golden brown. Do NOT overcook, as that would toughen the calamari. Remove from skillet and keep warm.

To skillet add 1 tablespoon of each of the following:
Diced tomatoes, seeds removed
Diced green onions
Finely chopped garlic
Diced shallots
Chopped parsley
Chopped fresh thyme

Then add:
Dash of salt
Dried chili peppers, to taste
Several drops fresh lemon juice

Arrange calamari strips on a serving platter or individual plates. Surround with vegetables and herbs and serve.

Felix's Restaurant

Felix Gonzalez came to the United States from Guadalajara, Spain, in 1961. He arrived in the Wood River Valley when he was 18 to work for the Union Pacific Railroad. Later, in 1992, after working in several local restaurants, he opened his own; Felix's Restaurant was relocated to his family home on First Avenue in Ketchum in 2001.

KEARSARGE SALMON SPREAD

FROM TERRY PALMER

7 ounces cooked salmon

8 ounces cream cheese

1 tablespoon lemon juice

1 tablespoon onion, grated

1 teaspoon horseradish

$1/_4$ teaspoon liquid smoke

$1/_2$ cup walnuts, chopped

3 tablespoons parsley, chopped

Combine salmon, cream cheese, lemon juice, onion, horseradish and liquid smoke in food processor or blender. Process until smooth. Stir in chopped nuts and parsley, and transfer to a crock.

Refrigerate until ready to serve.

Makes 2 cups.

Serve with bagels sliced into bite-size wedges.

Terry Palmer was a member of the US Ski Team and an Olympian in Sapporo, Japan. In 1972, he was the US National Slalom Champion.

After racing on the Pro circuit for 6 years, he coached the Sun Valley Ski Team and the US Ski Team. Terry continues to be involved in the ski world as a contributor and ski tester for SKI magazine.

CHILE CRAB WAN TON CUPS

16 won ton wrappers

2 tablespoons olive oil

$1/4$ cup green onion, minced

4 ounces green chiles, diced

6 ounces crab meat, cooked

1 tablespoon mayonnaise

1 tablespoon Dijon mustard

$1/2$ cup jack cheese with chiles, shredded

Ethnic Elegance

Lightly brush one side of each won ton skin with oil. Center each square, oiled-side down, on a muffin cup (using a small muffin tin). Gently press skin down to line cup smoothly; skin will extend above pan rim.

In an 8-inch frying pan over medium heat, stir $1/2$ teaspoon oil and onions until onions are limp, about 1 minute. Remove from heat. Stir in chiles,crab, mayonnaise and mustard. Fill each won ton cup equally with crabmixture. Sprinkle evenly with cheese. Bake in a 350°F oven until rims ofwon ton skins are golden and crisp, about 8-10 minutes. Lift from pan and serve hot.

If making up to one day ahead, let the crab cups cool out of the pan on a rack, then cover and chill. To reheat, set slightly apart on a baking sheet and bake in a 375°F oven until hot, about 6-8 minutes.

Makes 16 won ton cups.

During her 5-year jaunt as a chef on a privately owned sailing vessel that circumnavigated the globe, Gayle Nelson acquired many sumptuous, ethnic recipes. Back in her mountain home in the Wood River Valley, she caters small dinners and cocktail parties, sharing cuisine from the many exotic foreign ports she visited.

Gayle

WILD DUCK BREAST PATÉ

FROM JIM ELLISON

A variation of this recipe can be used with wild pheasant. Begin by partially smoking the whole pheasant for about 30 minutes, then roasting with water in the oven until done. Allow the meat to cool, then bone and proceed with same steps as with duck paté. The pheasant paté is delicious served with peach chutney!

4 large ducks or 6 smaller ducks

1 medium white onion

4 cloves fresh garlic

4 sprigs fresh basil

12 ounces cream cheese, room temperature

1 tablespoon mayonnaise

Tabasco or Mongolian fire sauce

Salt & pepper

Whole peppercorns or pistachio nuts, shells removed

Fillet breasts from whole ducks. (Use the remaining legs and bones to make a game stock that can be frozen and used for other game sauces.) In a frying pan, cook the breast fillets in canola or olive oil until done through. Remove and cool.

Using a food processor, mince the onion and garlic. Place in a large mixing bowl. Finely chop basil and add to the mixing bowl.

Put the cooled duck breasts into the food processor and mince until granular. (You may find a steel shot adding to the noise of the processor!) Remove the minced meat less the shot, add mayonnaise, then combine with onion, garlic and basil in the mixing bowl. Blend in softened cream cheese. Use a mixer or your hands to mix thoroughly. Add Tabasco or fire sauce, salt and pepper to taste. Mound mixture into two balls and place in the refrigerator, covered, until cold. (Overnight is fine if you are preparing ahead of time.)

For final presentation, remove the mixture from the refrigerator and add either peppercorns or pistachio nuts, or place in appropriate service crocks with a whole basil leaf on top. Garnish with fresh cilantro. Serve with crackers. Individual crocks can be covered with waxed paper and frozen for future use or as gifts.

Jim Ellison, of Ellison Machinery and Meritage Inc., has been a part-time resident of the Wood River Valley for 20 years. He and his family feel a great affection for the people and the spirit here. They enjoy all the outdoor and community opportunities, in all seasons. Cooking is a shared part of their family time. Jim has been cooking since childhood, and particularly enjoys the gathering and preparation of game birds and fish.

SPINACH BACON ROLL-UPS

FROM THE SUN VALLEY CENTER FOR THE ARTS

Our staff adores food and wine, and many of us are quite accomplished chefs. Busy schedules mean finding recipes that fit into the moments between work, kids and the next event. We love this recipe; it's quick, easy and tasty. We suggest serving these roll ups with a chilled Fumé Blanc or Sauvignon Blanc. Enjoy!

6 bacon slices

1 10-ounce package frozen spinach, chopped, thawed and squeezed dry

4 ounces cream cheese, room temperature

$1/4$ cup mayonnaise

1 teaspoon salt

$1/2$ teaspoon pepper

$1/2$ cup green onions, chopped

$1^1/_2$ tablespoons horseradish

3 9-inch-diameter flour tortillas

Cook bacon in large, heavy skillet over medium heat until crisp; drain. Crumble bacon into a medium bowl; stir in spinach and next 5 ingredients. Heat 1 tortilla in large skillet over high heat until warm and pliable (or in a towel in the microwave for 30 seconds), then transfer to a work surface. Spread $1/3$ of filling over tortilla, leaving $1/2$ inch border on edge. Roll up tightly, enclosing filling. Wrap in plastic. Repeat with the other 2 tortillas and remaining filling.

Chill for at least 1 hour, up to 4 hours.

Preheat oven to 400°F. Remove roll-ups from plastic; slice off unfilled ends. Cut crosswise on slight diagonal into $3/_4$-inch-thick slices. Arrange on a large baking sheet and bake until heated thoroughly, about 7 minutes.

Makes about 30 pieces.

The Sun Valley Center for the Arts is a non-profit arts organization whose mission is to stimulate and provoke the imagination while opening hearts and minds through excellence in diverse arts programming. The Center celebrated its 30th birthday in 2001 and is proud of all the events it has brought to the Valley over the past three decades, including children's and adults' classes, readings from nationally known writers, blues concerts, chamber music concerts, co-sponsored residencies with the Arden Trio, extensive in-school visits by artists and writers, a nationally recognized Arts and Crafts Festival, a documentary film festival, and free artist walk-throughs, slide shows and exhibitions. In twelve months, the Center's programs serve over 20,000 people, from the Wood River Valley and beyond!

All of these programs are made possible through the generosity of donors and members, and through the proceeds from the Center's only fundraiser, the Sun Valley Center Wine Auction, a four-day event held every July.

CAROLINA CRAB CAKES IN IDAHO

FROM CHEF C.K. AT EVERGREEN RESTAURANT

Carolina Crab Cakes:

1 tablespoon unsalted butter

$\frac{1}{2}$ cup yellow onions, diced $\frac{1}{8}$"

$\frac{1}{4}$ cup celery, diced $\frac{1}{8}$"

2 teaspoons serrano chile, diced

1 tablespoon garlic, minced

1 cup heavy cream

1 tablespoon Dijon mustard

1 pound crabmeat

1 cup panko
(Japanese breadcrumbs)

$\frac{1}{4}$ cup parsley

2 whole eggs

Creole Tartar Sauce:

3 tablespoons lemon juice

1 teaspoon chili powder
or Cajun spice mix

2 tablespoons Creole mustard

1 teaspoon salt

$\frac{1}{2}$ teaspoon black pepper

1 egg + 2 yolks

1 teaspoon Worcestershire sauce

$\frac{1}{2}$ cup green onions, thinly sliced

$\frac{1}{2}$ teaspoon soy sauce

$1\frac{1}{2}$ cups canola oil

$\frac{1}{4}$ cup dill pickle, chopped $\frac{1}{8}$"

1 tablespoon capers

Tabasco, to taste, if desired

Once upon a time, C.K. was known as the Evil Chef for his hot temper and sarcastic wit. In the nightly quest for perfection during the organized chaotic dance of fine cuisine preparation, these traits surfaced occasionally, so Evil he became, by name only.

After 25 years of experience, maturation, a perfect marriage to his pastry chef, Rebecca, two kids, thousands of miles of bicycle commuting, hundreds of hours of hang gliding and yoga practice, Evil has mellowed. The pursuit of perfection is going stronger than ever, and his accomplished cooking techniques have been enjoyed by many since 1985, when he became chef-partner with Jack Thornton at Evergreen. C.K.'s food philosophy is simple: He is not out to reinvent the wheel, just tweak it and make it truer and better!

Crab Cakes: Sweat the vegetables in butter in a heavy saucepan until soft, not browned. Add the cream, and reduce to half or a little less the original volume. Sauce should be thick. Cool in the refrigerator.

Combine the last 5 ingredients with the cooled vegetable cream. Using a $\frac{1}{4}$-cup measuring cup, form into cakes and completely cover with breadcrumbs. Fry in a little canola oil until golden brown. Serve with Creole Tartar Sauce. Makes 14 crab cakes.

Tartar Sauce: Combine everything except the last 4 ingredients in a food processor. Start it up and drizzle in the oil to make a mayonnaise. Add the final 3 items and pulse once or twice, just to combine very briefly. Serve with the crab cakes or use this sauce as a coleslaw dressing.

SPICY AHI CHOP-UP

FROM CHEF ANDREAS HEAPHY AT GLOBUS

Ahi Mix:

1 pound sushi-grade Ahi, finely chopped

1 teaspoon Sambal Oelek (or other chili paste)

2 tablespoons spring onion, finely chopped

1 tablespoon tobiko(flying fish roe, optional)

1 tablespoon pickled ginger, finely chopped

1 pinch Kosher salt

1 pinch freshly ground pepper

1 tablespoon Worcestershire sauce

2 tablespoons cucumber, peeled, de-seeded and finely chopped

Serves 4 as an appetizer.

For Serving:

Romaine hearts

Toasted sesame seeds

Tobiko

Daikon radish sprouts

Lemon wedges

Combine all Ahi Mix ingredients and let flavors marry for half an hour in the refrigerator.

To serve, arrange the romaine hearts on a platter and place 1 tablespoon of the Ahi mix onto each leaf. Garnish with the extra tobiko, sesame seeds, and daikon sprouts. Squeeze a lemon wedge above the platter just before serving.

PICKLED SALMON

FROM NANCY STONINGTON

I haven't cooked for years, so my husband feeds me! He collected this recipe from our good friend, Frank Hill, in Naknek, Alaska. Frank is a native of Bristol Bay, half Aleut and half Finnish, and a lifelong Bristol Bay commercial fisherman. This old, native-Alaskan family recipe is very easy to prepare, and it's great with crackers!

3-4 fresh salmon fillets (preferably Bristol Bay Red Salmon)

2 large white onions

1 box pickling spices

1 quart white vinegar

1 small jar sweet pickles

Canning jars (2 quart to 1 gallon) or large ceramic bowls

Remove the skin by laying the fish on a flat board, skin side down. Press a fillet or other sharp knife between the skin and the flesh of the fish, starting at the head end and sliding the knife along the fillet.

Cut the fish into bite-size pieces, $1/4$" thick by 1" square, cutting across the grain of the fish.

Next, cut the onion into slices or rings approximately $1/8$" thick.

In a jar or bowl, place a layer of onion, sprinkle some pickling spices over it, then add a layer of salmon. Repeat until you run out of salmon. Put a final layer of onion and spices on top.

Divide the liquid from the sweet pickles among your jars or bowls. Cover entirely with vinegar and put in the refrigerator for 4 or 5 days. (Taste it after a day or so to see if it needs more spices or vinegar.) Once a day, stir and mix your concoction.

Serve with your favorite crackers.

Nancy Taylor Stonington, watercolorist, came to the Valley in 1971. She lived north of Ketchum and operated the Stonington Gallery in Ketchum for over 27 years. She and her husband, Chuck Beatie, now travel between Alaska, Washington, Oregon and Idaho, where Nancy paints on location and from her studio on Vashon Island. The Stonington Gallery in Seattle features Nancy's original paintings and prints.

Nancy Stonington

CROSTINI WITH TOMATOES

FROM NANCY FERRIES AND HER FAMOUS POTATOES

I adopted this crowd-pleaser from Bee, my next door neighbor in the Gorge. It's great apres windsurfing or anytime. Enjoy!

12 $\frac{1}{4}$-inch thick slices French baguette

Olive oil

$\frac{1}{4}$ cup pesto (or more if you like)

3 $\frac{1}{2}$-ounce log plain goat cheese, such as Montrachet

$\frac{3}{4}$ cup diced ripe tomatoes

2 green onions, chopped

Tabasco

Preheat oven to 350°F. Arrange bread slices on baking sheet, and brush them lightly with olive oil. Bake until brown and crisp, about 10 minutes. Cool and let stand at room temperature.

Spread pesto on each baguette slice. Place a thin slice of goat cheese on top. Add diced tomatoes, then a few green onions. And last but not least, add a dash of Tabasco.

For the new century, Nancy Ferries has revived the classic "Famous Potato" logo that first adorned Sun Valley t-shirts and hats in 1979. So look out for that lovable pair of spuds in local shops!

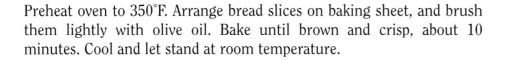

DANGEROUS EGGNOG

This recipe is great for holiday parties—
but don't let anyone drink too much, or they will be sleeping over!

13 eggs

2 pounds super-fine sugar

1 quart bourbon

1 quart dark rum

1 pint cognac or brandy

1 ½ pints milk

3 ½ pints heavy cream

Nutmeg

Serves 30.

Separate egg whites and yolks. In a very large bowl, beat eggs yolks; gradually stir in sugar. Slowly pour in bourbon, rum, cognac, milk and cream.

Whip egg whites and gently fold into mixture just before serving. Ladle into cups and sprinkle with nutmeg. Enjoy!

You can make this eggnog (minus the egg whites) days in advance, letting it ferment. Be sure to stir it daily. This will make it very smooth. Add whipped egg whites just before serving.

Recipe can be halved.

Muffy Davis grew up ski racing in the Wood River Valley. As a child, her dream was to ski race in the Olympics. But when she was 16, a downhill training accident that left Muffy paralyzed from the mid-chest down seemed to crush that dream. Initially devastated, she refocused her energy on education and went on to graduate from Stanford University. Muffy then decided to get back into ski racing, this time with the US Disabled Alpine Ski Team. In 1998, she accomplished her childhood dream and won a Bronze medal in the Paralympics in Nagano, Japan. Muffy now has over ten World Cup victories, including a World Championship in 2000 and Overall World Cup Title. Muffy is training for the 2002 Paralympics in Park City, Utah, where she hopes to bring home the Gold!

Growing up, Muffy loathed the smallness of our valley because she couldn't get away with anything; but after her accident, she came to appreciate our close-knit community. She feels lucky to have grown up in Sun Valley, the place she will always call "home."

NIGHT-TIME ORGANIC TEA

FROM DEBBIE EDGERS STURGES

Mint and chamomile grow very well in the mountains, and both will thrive in a shady spot in the garden. Each fall I harvest my herbs. I tie the mint together in bunches and hang them from a beam in my house. I pick the chamomile flowers and put them into a shallow basket. When the mint and chamomile are dry, I store them in separate jars. The herbs I grow in my garden make a very delicious, calming, organic drink before bedtime. I enjoy a cup almost every night, and pour the remainder of the tea into a glass pitcher to put into the refrigerator for iced tea the next day. Leave the chamomile out if you want a more energetic drink.

5 3-inch sprigs of true peppermint
or spearmint

2 teaspoons of chamomile flowers

Put the herbs into a preheated teapot. Pour boiling water into the pot and let it steep for 10 minutes.

Debbie Edgers Sturges came to the Valley in 1973 and discovered a growing art community. She stayed to pursue the two activities she loves most: painting and skiing. In the winter, she can be found in her studio, on the North Valley Ski Trails or on Baldy. In the summer, she's either painting, hiking or in her garden. She's always looking for local wildlife, a new ski or hiking trail, a new garden to design and new artistic boundaries to push.

Debbie and her husband, Brian, enjoy get-togethers with the friends and family that make this valley such a special place.

BREAKFAST & BREADS

SAWTOOTH GRANOLA

FROM CHRISTIN COOPER

A good friend living in Triumph passed this recipe on to me in the early 1970s. It powered the two of us through many a Sawtooth scramble in the old days, and many a buzzer-to-buzzer Baldy powder day. For years, I carried stashes of it with me to Europe, squirreled away in ski bags, meant for fueling pre-dawn slalom raids on the World Cup. Problem was, we'd all end up dipping in by the handful halfway through our ten-hour drive across Northern Italy, or passing the time during long afternoon blizzards, or while waiting for the fog to lift or training to resume. The stash never lasted!

Preheat oven to 325°F

In a 9x13 baking pan, melt over low heat until combined:

$^3/_4$ cup oil (preferably cold-pressed sunflower or canola)

$^3/_4$ cup honey

Remove from heat & add:

2 cups rolled oats

1 cup wheat flakes

1 cup barley flakes

1 cup Grape Nuts

$^1/_2$ cup wheat germ

$^1/_2$ cup sesame seeds

$^1/_2$ cup sunflower seeds

$^1/_4$ cup pumpkin seeds

$^1/_4$ cup poppy or chia seeds

Remove from oven & add:

$^1/_2$ cup raisins

$^1/_4$ cup chopped dates

$^1/_2$ cup chopped or whole almonds, cashews or hazelnuts
(or another dried fruit)

Mix until all ingredients are well coated. Bake for 15-20 minutes, stirring once halfway through to keep grains at the edges from getting fried.

Let cool in pans. Pull the granola apart into chewy hunks to store in bags or jars.

This recipe can easily be doubled or tripled, simplified or elaborated, depending on your budget, your mood, or what's in the pantry.

Christin Cooper grew up in Ketchum, skiing for the Sun Valley Ski Team, and in 1977, went on to join the US Ski Team. In the 1982 World Championships, she became the first and only American triple medalist in alpine skiing, and in the 1984 Olympics, she won a silver medal in giant slalom. Christin and her husband, Mark Taché, mountain climb, rock climb, and ski as much as is humanly possible on mountains all over the world, but Christin claims that Baldy rules!

Christin Cooper

GRANOLA

FROM TOM BROKAW

Pitted dates, prunes, raisins or other dried fruit

4 cups old-fashioned oatmeal

1 cup shredded coconut

1 cup pine nuts or walnuts

1 cup wheat germ

$1/3$ cup sesame seeds

$1/2$ cup honey

$1/2$ cup oil

Tom Brokaw, Anchor and Managing Editor of *NBC Nightly News,* has an impressive history of "firsts": the first exclusive US one-on-one interview with Mikhail Gorbachev; the only anchor to report from the scene the night the Berlin Wall fell; the first American anchor to conduct an interview with the Dalai Lama; the first network evening news anchor to report from the site of the Oklahoma City bombing; the first American television interview with Russian President Vladimir Putin.

Snip dates/prunes/raisins into small pieces and set aside.

In a large bowl, combine oatmeal, coconut, nuts, wheat germ and sesame seeds.

In a saucepan, stir in honey and oil and bring to a boil. Remove from heat and stir into the oatmeal mixture; mix well.

Spread new mixture into two 10" x 15" baking pans and bake for 25 minutes at 325°F, stirring occasionally.

Let cool, and add fruit.

Makes approximately $1^{1}/_{2}$ pounds of granola.

And it was Tom Brokaw who addressed us calmly but effectively to report the tragedy of September 11, 2001 when America was attacked by terrorists. It's no wonder he has received so many awards for his extraordinary work, including a Peabody and seven Emmys. Tom Brokaw is equally at ease whether he is covering news events that make history or visiting Sun Valley.

MOLASSES PANCAKES

FROM ALISON KIESEL

Alison and her daughter Kaelin.

$^1/_4$ cup oatmeal

1 $^1/_2$ - 1 $^3/_4$ cups buttermilk

1 cup whole wheat flour

$^1/_4$ cup bran

1 tablespoon lecithin granules

1 teaspoon baking soda

2 egg white, beaten

1 tablespoon medium unsulfured molasses

Mix oats and buttermilk. Place the dry ingredients in a large bowl, breaking up any lumps, and stirring until combined. Beat the egg whites.

Heat a skillet to hot, and oil lightly. Add the oats and buttermilk, molasses and egg whites to the dry ingredients. Mix well. (Use more or less buttermilk depending on your desired thickness.)

Pour on the hot skillet to make your pancakes, and serve with warm maple syrup and fresh fruit.

This makes enough for one hungry person or two light eaters!

Alison Owen Kiesel was the first woman to race in the US Nordic Junior Nationals and the only woman to win a Nordic World Cup. She's also a two-time Olympian and six-time National Champion. Alison manages Thunder Spring Nordic, and she loves to cross-country ski nearly every day in the winter and mountain bike and run on our awesome trails in the summer. She has two children who are both US Nordic Junior National Champions.

Alison Owen Kiesel

MOUNTAIN HIGH PANCAKES

FROM LYNN TONERI & R.C. HINK

Mix in a blender or with an electric mixer:

3 eggs

$^2/_3$ cup flour

$^2/_3$ cup milk

$^1/_4$ teaspoon cinnamon

$^1/_2$ teaspoon vanilla

After blending, add:

$^1/_4$ to $^1/_3$ cup dried cranberries

Melt $^1/_4$ cup butter or margarine in an 8- or 9-inch deep baking dish. Pour in batter and bake at 425°F for 15-20 minutes. Pancake will rise 6 inches or so and be a golden brown when done.

Top with your favorite sliced fruit and pour on maple and coconut syrup.

Lynn belongs to the newest generation of outdoor watercolorists, painting whatever it is she happens to be doing: "If I'm skindiving, I paint tropical fish. Canoeing, waterfowl; hiking, wildlife. And if relaxing, I paint the flowers and birds I see in my backyard in Hailey."

R.C. finds inspiration for his wood sculptures in the majesty of the mountains and the wilderness of the West. He plays with functional and nonfunctional forms in wood, and many find humor in his creations.

Locals and visitors of the Wood River Valley enjoy the artistic creations of Lynn Toneri and R.C. Hink. Both genres are offered at Lynn's Ketchum gallery and in R.C.'s Bellevue studio.

SUNDAY SWEDISH PANCAKES

FROM ANDY MUNTER

I found and simplified this recipe in the mid-'80s. After my first serving, I was rewarded by warm memories of Grandma Munter making these same pancakes on the farmhouse wood cook stove in the mid-'50s. We would beg her for pancakes but she would only agree to make them if my older brother would split a bunch of kindling to get the fire hot enough. Her pancakes were even better mixed in her big bowl with her large whisk. We called them "Grandma Pancakes," and they are the easiest pancakes you will ever make!

3 eggs

1 cup white flour

1 $^3/_4$ cup milk

1 tablespoon oil

Put the eggs and milk in a blender and mix, then add the flour and oil and mix again. If possible, cook the pancakes on a cast iron skillet, hot and fast. Top with lots of butter and pure maple syrup.

Andy Munter first saw Ketchum on a wet and foggy June night in 1977. While travelling the west looking for a good resort to spend the winter. He pulled up to Su Casa (now the Ketchum Grill) for dinner. Leaning against the picket fence was an old beater bike and sitting on the seat was a big black bird. It croaked "All Right!" and flew off into the rainy night. How could he ignore that and not stay in Ketchum?

Since 1980, Andy has helped a lot of people fulfill their dreams in the outdoors as salesman, manager, partner and owner of Backwoods Mountain Sports. He's a member of the Winter Coalition, helping to solve motorized/non-motorized winter conflict in a collaborative way, and he's on the Board of Idaho River United, a grassroots, statewide group committed to protecting existing wild rivers and restoring degraded watersheds and fisheries.

WILD MUSHROOM FRITTATA

FROM STEVE MINER

One of the many things I love to do in Sun Valley is hunt for the morel mushrooms that arrive every spring around Mothers Day at various sites up and down the Wood River. They are among the most delicious of wild mushrooms, but if you have no luck finding any or don't want to spend the exorbitant price they command at the market, common grocery store mushrooms will make an acceptable substitute for this frittata. There are other excellent wild mushrooms that grow in our area, but make sure of your identification, as a mistake could prove deadly!

3 tablespoons extra virgin olive oil

2 cups onion, thinly sliced

12 morel mushrooms, chopped

salt

5 eggs

$2/3$ cup freshly grated Parmigiano-Reggiano cheese

Black pepper, freshly ground

2 tablespoons butter

Put the oil, onions, mushrooms, and some salt in a large sauté pan. Turn heat to med/low and sauté until the mushrooms have cast off all their water and the onions are a golden brown. Set aside.

Turn on the broiler to preheat.

Crack the eggs into a mixing bowl and beat until the yolks and whites are well mixed. Add the mushrooms and onions, draining them of oil by transferring them with a slotted spoon. Add the cheese, a pinch or two of salt and several grindings of pepper. Mix all ingredients well so they are evenly distributed.

Put the butter in a skillet (I find a 10" nonstick works the best) and melt the butter on med/high heat. When the butter foams, add the egg mixture and turn the heat down to very low. Let cook - NO STIRRING - until the eggs are set. This will take a little while, as a frittata is supposed to cook slowly.

Finally, when only the very top is still a little runny, stick the pan under the broiler to finish it off.

Slide the whole frittata onto a plate, cut into wedges like a pie and serve. This tastes just as good cold or at room temperature as it does hot!

Steve Miner directed such features as *Friday the 13th Parts 2* and *3*, *Soul Man*, *Wild Hearts Can't Be Broken*, *Halloween H2O*, *Forever Young*, and *Texas Rangers*. His television credits include *Kate Brasher*, *The Practice*, *Chicago Hope*, and *The Wonder Years*, which was nominated for an Emmy for Outstanding Directing in a Comedy Series.

Steve is pictured here at his Warm Springs cabin, trying to identify the various mushrooms he found earlier that morning.

Steve Miner

COPPER RIVER SOCKEYE GRAVLAX

FROM RIC LUM

This is delicious for breakfast on a bagel with goat cheese, but can also be served as an appetizer on crackers with crème fraîche and chives.

1 $\frac{1}{2}$ tablespoons kosher salt

1 tablespoon brown sugar

1 pound center-cut Copper River Sockeye Salmon

1 teaspoon lemon zest

$\frac{3}{4}$ cup Italian parsley, chopped

Freshly ground pepper

1 $\frac{1}{2}$ tablespoons grappa, vodka or schnapps

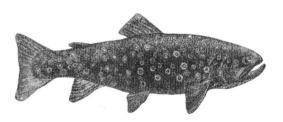

Combine the salt and sugar in a small bowl. Set fish fillet skin-side down on a large sheet of plastic wrap. Rub salt and sugar mix evenly over both sides of fish.

Combine lemon zest, parsley, ground pepper and grappa. Roll the fillet in mixture.

Wrap the fillet in plastic and put package in a skillet; top with a smaller skillet and put 4 pounds of weight on top to press it down. Refrigerate 36-48 hours. Turn package once and wrap the fish in fresh plastic, after draining any excess liquid.

Use a boning knife or very sharp chef's knife to slice very thinly ($\frac{1}{8}$-inch). Serve for breakfast on a bagel with goat cheese.

With a passion for cooking and eating great food, Ric Lum has been catering and offering cooking classes for over twenty years. He loves using traditional, heirloom Asian and Italian recipes and has spent much time learning from noted chefs around the world, but he also offers wonderful Rocky Mountain specialties.

In his spare time, Ric lets his creative energies flow to his artwork, shown above!

GLORY MUFFINS

FROM BBQ BOB MAXEY

This is one of my mother's recipes!

2 cups flour

$1^1/_4$ cups sugar

2 teaspoons baking soda

2 teaspoons cinnamon

$^1/_2$ teaspoon salt

2 cups grated carrots

$^1/_2$ cup raisins

$^1/_2$ cup nuts (your choice)

1 peeled, grated apple

3 eggs

1 cup oil

2 teaspoons vanilla

In a mixing bowl, sift flour, sugar, soda, cinnamon and salt. Stir in carrots, raisins, nuts and apple.

In another bowl, beat the eggs, and mix with oil and vanilla. Add the dry ingredients and stir until just mixed.

Pour into greased muffin tins and bake at 350°F for 30-35 minutes until golden brown.

Barbeque Bob was born an airforce brat in Guam and educated worldwide. He graduated from San Francisco Art Institute in 1972 and took up the expatriate life in Australia, selling his underground comics collection for airfare. After a stint in Redondo Beach, Bob moved to Idaho in 1976. He has been playing with the BoBo's and fishing ever since!

Barbeque Bob

SLEEP-OVER COFFE CAKE

FROM LARRY FLYNN

This is a great timesaver when entertaining houseguests. They will not only wake up feeling refreshed from your fine accommodations, but the smell of this coffee cake is an added bonus! Enjoy, and in vino veritas!

Cake:

2 cups flour

1 cup sugar

1 cup buttermilk

$^2/_3$ cup butter
or margarine, softened

$^1/_2$ cup brown sugar

2 large eggs

2 tablespoons dry
milk powder

1 tablespoon cinnamon

1 teaspoon baking soda

1 teaspoon baking powder

$^1/_2$ teaspoon salt

Topping:

$^1/_2$ cup brown sugar

$^1/_2$ cup walnuts or pecans,
chopped

$^1/_2$ teaspoon nutmeg

$^1/_4$ cup butter or margarine,
melted

1 cup berries — optional
(I like huckleberries or
blueberries)

Grease and flour a 9x13 baking pan. Combine all cake ingredients in a large mixing bowl. Mix at low speed until well blended. Pour into your prepared pan. Mix all dry topping ingredients and sprinkle evenly over the batter. Refrigerate overnight and enjoy your houseguests' company (and the wine they brought)!

The next morning, drizzle cake batter and topping with melted butter, top with berries if desired, and place in preheated 350°F oven. Bake for 30 minutes, or until top is a rich, golden brown. Cool for at least 15 minutes and serve warm with coffee, water and aspirin (if it was cheap wine!).

Long-time Valley resident Larry W. Flynn has been active in our community since he moved here in 1986. He has been the fund-raising auctioneer for the Advocates, the Sagebrush Equine Handicapped Riding Program, the Animal Shelter, the Hospital Auxiliary, Expedition Inspiration and the Sun Valley Wine Auction. Larry travels the country working for others, including the Christopher Reeve Paralysis Foundation, the Self Family Arts Center and Acker Merrill in New York. In his "spare" time, Larry is General Manager for Alpine Broadcasting and he participates on the Board of Directors for the Bill Janss Community Center project. Larry lives in Hailey with his wife, Christy, and their two children, Jackson and Rita. They love to hike, snow ski, water ski and golf. Opportunities to relocate abound, but Larry prefers to stay right here!

MONKEY BREAD

FROM RICH & ROSIE FELDHEIM

4 cans refrigerator biscuit dough, cut into fourths

$^2/_3$ cup sugar

1 tablespoon cinnamon

Syrup Mixture

1 $^1/_2$ sticks butter

$^1/_2$ cup sugar

$^1/_2$ cup brown sugar

1 teaspoon cinnamon

Mix sugar and cinnamon and roll into dough. (You can also layer in chopped walnuts or add raisins if desired!)

Place in a greased bundt pan and pour the syrup mixture over the top. Bake in a 350°F oven for approximately 20 mintues or until the biscuits are golden brown.

Rosie Feldheim

Rich Feldheim is a lawyer and CPA who, friends claim, turns everything he touches to gold! He is President of Abby's Pizza, which has 36 restaurants in the Northwest. He's also President of Star Resorts International, which develops private residence clubs. Rosie is one of Jackie Sorenson's original aerobics instructors and is still teaching. The Feldheims have been visiting Sun Valley for twenty years; this is where they learned to ski. After a lot of winter visits, they started spending their summers here and finally bought a little piece of quiet and beauty in Croy Canyon, where they come to unwind.

STOVE-TOP SEAWATER BREAD

FROM DR. SCOTT & BARBARA EARL

Long ago, in the 1960s before bread makers, we saw this recipe in The New York Times. *It's meant for small, ovenless, ocean-going boats and uses straight, unadulterated seawater. It's fun, easy, adaptable, and it makes wonderful bread. Seawater is a bit short in supply here in Idaho, so you'll want to add enough salt to the water to make it taste like seawater — a heaping teaspoon works just fine!*

1 $\frac{1}{2}$ cups warm water

1 heaping teaspoon salt

1 tablespoon sugar

1 tablespoon (1 packet) dried yeast

4 cups all-purpose flour

Mix together and stir well. The original recipe says that kneading is not necessary, but kneading makes it easier to mix!

Grease and flour a heavy pan. (We use a pressure cooker and leave the valve open, but a heavy, covered sauce pan or small Dutch oven works fine. We have also used an aluminum camp pot over a camp stove for making this bread.)

Add the dough, cover the pan, set aside in a warm place for two hours.

Cook, covered, over low heat on top of the stove for half an hour. (You may have to experiment. A setting low and medium works best on our stove—the crust should be browned, but not burned.) Turn bread over and cook for another half-hour.

We have tried many permutations. We have used rye, buckwheat and whole-wheat flour, mixed with all-purpose flour in various combinations. All work fine. Rolling the dough in granola before placing it in the pan gives the bread a crispy crust.

Before submitting this recipe, we tried olive-rosemary bread: $\frac{1}{2}$ cup pitted and chopped Calamata olives, $\frac{3}{4}$ teaspoon crushed rosemary, 1 cup whole wheat flour, 3 cups white flour, greasing the pan with olive oil and butter...it was delicious! Give it a try!

Dr. Scott Earle first came to Sun Valley in 1956 as a surgical resident-in-training. The Sun Valley Hospital was then quartered on the third floor of the Sun Valley Lodge. In 1959, Scott and Barbara joined the staff full-time, Scott as a general surgeon, Barbara an OR and staff nurse. One thing led to another and they were married three years later! In 1970, they left the Valley for Ohio where Scott worked his way up the academic ladder at Cleveland's Case Western University School of Medicine and Barbara raised their four children. Every year, they visited Sun Valley, and finally returned to spend their summers after Dr. Earle retired as Professor of Surgery, Emeritus, in 1991.

Scott has always hiked and climbed our mountains, photographing the rich variety of wildflowers that grow here, an endeavor that culminated in the publication of *Idaho Mountain Wildflowers: A Photographic Compendium*, released in 2001.

SOUPS, SALADS & SANDWICHES

Fresh Greens & Balsamic Vinaigrette

FROM ZACH CRIST

This recipe is compliments of cinematographer John Stephens.

$2/3$ cup olive oil

$1/3$ cup balsamic vinegar

2 tablespoons soy sauce

Dash of fish sauce

1 teaspoon crushed, dried chili peppers

1 heaping tablespoon brown sugar

1 tablespoon minced garlic

Toss with fresh, homegrown lettuce and serve.

Sun Valley is hometown to Zach Crist, who grew up skiing. He was a member of the US Ski Team and World Cup Team, and 1996 North American Champion. Since retiring from the World Cup circuit in 1998, Zach has shifted his focus to freeskiing, where he has become one of the sport's most prominent figures. After four medals in four appearances last season, Zach has proven to be the most dominant force in the world of skier cross. Together, Zach and his brother Reggie have never been denied a podium finish – at least one of them has reached the top three in every skier cross they have entered over the last three seasons.

The Crist brothers are part owners and operators of Equator Productions, makers of adventure documentaries. After creating a partnership with Outdoor Life Network and Men's Journal Magazine, Equator has delivered four films in the last year. Zach admits that working with his older brother has been key to his own success. He hopes to keep the synergy alive as he prepares to defend his title at the Winter X Games in February of 2002.

SALAD NICOISE

FROM MARIEL HEMINGWAY

In honor of my dad, you can make this an Asian Nicoise. Instead of green beans, use snow peas. Cut the olives and anchovies, and add sesame seeds and water chestnuts. Sear the ahi as directed below, but use canola oil and tamari sauce. For the dressing, mix some wasabi, $1/4$ teaspoon tamari sauce and lemon with 1 tablespoon sesame oil and 1 tablespoon canola oil.

16 green beans, ends trimmed

2 large red potatoes, peeled or not

1 head Boston lettuce, washed and torn into large pieces

2 hardboiled eggs, sliced into quarters lengthwise

$1/2$ cup Greek green or black olives

1 tablespoon capers, drained and rinsed

13 ounces fresh ahi tuna steak or canned tuna
(but the fresh tastes best!)

2 medium quartered tomatoes

1 ounce canned flat anchovy fillets, drained (optional)

1 tablespoon fresh basil, chopped

1 tablespoon scallions, minced

Oil and vinegar to taste

Serves 4.

Boil or steam the green beans until barely tender, approximately 5 minutes. Drain and rinse under cold water, then slice diagonally into 1-inch sections.

Cook potatoes in same pot or steamer 15-20 minutes. Cut into 1-inch cubes. Sprinkle with oil and vinegar while they are still warm. Set aside.

To cook the fresh ahi, heat a non-stick skillet with a little olive oil and get the skillet very hot. Put the whole tuna steak into the skillet for 2 minutes on each side for rare, longer if rare tuna (sushi grade) scares you. Slice tuna into cubes or long, rectangular slices.

Line a large platter with lettuce leaves. Arrange green beans, potatoes, hardboiled eggs, olives, capers, tuna, tomatoes and anchovies on top of the lettuce. Sprinkle with basil and scallions. Spoon oil and vinegar to taste over the salad or serve on the side. Serve immediately.

Mariel Hemingway is a familiar face in Sun Valley, and she always has a smile for those who see her in the market or on the trails. She attended local schools and has always been a part of our community. For all of her accomplishments, including many starring film roles and an Oscar nomination in Woody Allen's movie *Manhattan*, Mariel Hemingway is not concerned about box-office acclaim; she simply enjoys acting, which offers her the flexibility to be with her children. Having recently completed two new films for HBO and reprised her role as a Secret Service agent in *Hidden Target*, a sequel to *First Daughter*, Mariel plans to direct *A Moveable Feast*, based on a novel written by her granddaddy, Ernest. "Going into directing is a natural for me — I love being organized, and love the process of making it all come together."

Mariel Hemingway

WILD RICE & LOBSTER SALAD

FROM JIMMIE HEUGA

1 cup wild rice

3 cups water

Cook rice until tender, about 20 minutes, to make $3^{1}/_{2}$ cups rice.

Combine rice with the following and set aside:

2 cups lobster meat, cooked and cut up

2 avocados, sprinkled with 1 tablespoon lemon juice
to prevent discoloring

$^{1}/_{2}$ cup red onion, diced finely

Vinaigrette:

1 tablespoon Dijon mustard

$2^{1}/_{2}$ tablespoons red wine vinegar

$^{1}/_{4}$ cup peanut oil

$^{1}/_{4}$ cup olive oil

$^{1}/_{4}$ teaspoon garlic, minced

2 tablespoons parsley, chopped

Salt & pepper to taste

In a small bowl, mix the mustard and vinegar. Add the oils slowly to emulsify. Next add the garlic, parsley, salt and pepper.

To finish, mix the vinaigrette with the rice and lobster mixture.
Serve at room temperature.

More than 35 years after he won an Olympic skiing medal, Jimmie Heuga still is being recognized for greatness. Diagnosed with multiple sclerosis shortly after retiring from the US Ski Team in 1968, Jimmie was advised by doctors to conserve his strength and "wait for a cure." But the youngest male ever to make the US Ski Team instead continued to participate in a variety of activities. After dedicating the first half of his life to skiing, Heuga's focus shifted to assisting the physically challenged; and in 1984, he opened the Jimmie Heuga Center, which provides medical, rehabilitative and educational programs while focusing on wellness and encouraging people to have active lives. Although the Center was initially designed to help victims of MS, an incurable disease, Heuga's current vision is to assist anyone with a physical challenge. A major fundraising event for the Center is The Jimmie Heuga Ski Express, held annually in ski resorts across America, including here in Sun Valley.

SPICY ORIENTAL CHICKEN SALAD

FROM MARY ANN MIX

No matter the season, when my daughter comes home to Hailey for a visit, she always expects her favorite dish. Fortunately, it's simple and nourishing!

Salad:

4 steamed, skinless, boneless chicken breasts, trimmed and thinly sliced on diagonal

8 ounces soba (buckwheat) noodles or thin spaghetti, cooked, drained and chilled

1½ cups fresh pea pods or blanched green beans

2 cucumbers, thinly sliced into strips

1 cup tomato wedges

4 scallions, sliced on bias

1½ cups carrots, cut into thin strips

4 cups mixed salad greens

Crispy Chinese noodles

1 cup toasted peanuts

Dressing:

½ cup rice wine vinegar

3 tablespoons reduced-sodium soy sauce

2 tablespoons sesame oil

2 tablespoons fresh ginger root, minced or grated

2 teaspoons Thai chili paste

2 teaspoons honey

4-5 cloves garlic, minced

2 tablespoons vegetable oil

In 1983, Mary Ann Mix, along with Dorothy Moore ("Aunt Dottie"), was elected to the Hailey City Council and became the first women ever to be so honored. In 1996, Mary Ann became the first woman in Blaine County's history to be elected to the Board of Commissioners, and in 1999, she became the first woman to be elected as Chairman of the Blaine County Commissioners. In addition to working for her community, Mary Ann owns and operates an environmental consulting business, MPE, Inc.

Blend dressing ingredients until gingerroot and garlic are fully incorporated. Spoon 2 tablespoons dressing over cooked noodles. Add chicken, veggies and greens, and toss with remaining dressing. Garnish with crispy noodles and peanuts, and serve.

Buon appetito!
mary mix

FLAMING BURNS A.K.A FLAMING SPINACH SALAD

FROM BOBBIE BURNS

Salad:

8 ounces spinach, fresh

$1/2$ pound bacon, cooked

Red onion, chopped

Mushrooms, sliced

Croutons (optional)

Dressing:

Juice from one lemon

2 tablespoons sugar

6 tablespoons olive oil

2 tablespoons red wine vinegar

Seasoning:

Big dash of Worcestershire

Salt & pepper

Parsley

Tarragon

Serves 2-4.

Combine salad. Heat dressing, then toss in salad. Heat $1/3$ cup brandy. Just before it boils, ignite at table. Pour onto salad and toss!

bobbie with his daughter.

Bobbie Burns is best spotted driving through Ketchum in his 1957 Willys. He was a champion ski racer and freestyler, and manufacturer of The Ski in the early 1970s. Bobbie designs elegant yet casual clothing through his label, bobbie burns company, which can be found in his shops in Sun Valley and Park City.

FABULOUS POTATO SALAD

FROM SCOTT & CAROL GLENN

6 large potatoes, boiled, cooled and cut into chunks

$3/4$ cup mayonnaise

$1/6$ cup red wine vinegar

1 tablespoon Coleman's dry mustard

2 tablespoons honey

Salt & pepper to taste

2 hardboiled eggs, chopped (optional)

$1/4$ cup onions, chopped

Fresh parsley, chopped

Scott Glenn has played leading roles in such highly acclaimed films such as *Urban Cowboy, The Right Stuff, Silverado, The Hunt for Red October, Backdraft* and *Silence of the Lambs*. Most recently, he appeared as the guru climber in *Vertical Limit*. He has also been a nominee for a Drama Desk Award, and the recipient of a Drama League Award for best actor, in the off-Broadway production of "Killer Joe." Carol Glenn, a nationally known artist, recently received a Moonhole Fellowship. She has exhibited her expressionistic oils and watercolors locally.

Cut up the potatoes and set aside. In a bowl, mix the mayonnaise, vinegar, mustard, honey, salt and pepper. Add the potatoes and toss. Add the eggs and onions and toss again. Sprinkle with parsley and serve.

Scott and Carol have called Ketchum home since 1978 and are very community-involved. They have helped raise money for Blaine County Search & Rescue, Alliance for the Wild Rockies, and The Advocates. They enjoy as many outdoor activities as possible, and love to ski, hike, motorcycle, mountain bike, rollerblade and shoot on the target range.

Scott Glenn

Carol Glenn

SPINACH & BLUE CHEESE SALAD WITH SLICED APPLES & SPICED CARMELIZED PECANS

FROM WOLFGANG PUCK

We are lucky to have this wonderful recipe courtesy of Wolfgang Puck. It is also available in his books, Pizza, Pasta & More! *and* Adventures in the Kitchen.

Salad:

1 apple, chilled

Juice of 1 small lemon

8 ounces spinach, washed thoroughly dried and stemmed

1 small head of radicchio (about 3 ounces), cut into chiffonade

5 ounces blue cheese, crumbled

Kosher salt and freshly ground white pepper

About $1/2$ cup Spago House Dressing (recipe below)

$1 1/2$ cups Spiced Caramelized Pecans (recipe below)

Serves 4.

Spago House Salad Dressing:
Whisk together, cover and refrigerate until needed.

2 large shallots, minced (1 heaping tablespoon)

1 tablespoon Dijon mustard

2 tablespoons zinfandel vinegar

2 tablespoons sherry wine vinegar

$1/2$ cup olive oil

$1/2$ cup vegetable oil

Salt

Freshly ground white pepper

Spiced Caramelized Pecans:

3 cups peanut oil

2 cups pecan halves

1 teaspoon Kosher salt

$1/2$ teaspoon cayenne pepper

1 cup sifted confectioner's sugar

One of an influential breed of chef-restaurateurs in America, Wolfgang Puck is credited with reviving California's culinary heritage. Blending fresh California ingredients and classical French training, his innovations in cooking have been enjoyed and praised by world leaders, Hollywood stars and fellow chefs alike.

Austrian-born Puck began his formal training at age 14, perhaps inspired by his mother, a hotel chef. Wolfgang came to the United States in 1973 and within a short time was the star attraction at Ma Maison in Los Angeles, as both chef and part owner. After publishing his first cookbook, *Modern French Cooking*, Puck left French cuisine to establish Spago Hollywood on the Sunset Strip. Over its eighteen years, Spago has earned many awards, including the prestigious Restaurant of the Year Award from the James Beard Foundation in 1994. In 1998, Wolfgang received the James Beard Foundation Award for Outstanding Chef.

Wolfgang, along with his wife and partner, Barbara Lazaroff, have since opened restaurants in many notable settings. Wolfgang continues to delight us with his culinary secrets!

Pecans: In a deep fryer or a deep pot, heat the oil to 350°F. In a large saucepan, bring 2 quarts of water to a boil, add pecans and boil for 2 minutes. Drain in a large strainer, sprinkle with salt and cayenne pepper, then coat with confectioner's sugar, a little at a time, so the sugar melts into the pecans. Shake the strainer to toss and coat the nuts until all sugar is used and all nuts are coated. Do not use your hands or a spoon to toss! Carefully add the nuts to the heated oil, keeping the oil at 350°F. Cook until golden brown, about 3 minutes, stirring occasionally. Remove with a slotted spoon to a baking tray and cool.

Salad: Cut the apple into quarters, remove the stem and seeds, and cut into very thin slices. Sprinkle with lemon juice and set aside. When ready to serve, in a salad bowl, combine the apple, spinach, radicchio and blue cheese. Season lightly with salt and pepper and toss with the dressing. Adjust seasonings to taste. To serve, divide the salad among 4 plates and sprinkle the pecans around each salad.

STANDBY GREEK SALAD

FROM TOM DROUGAS

This mix will keep in the refrigerator for a couple of days and can be served over a bed of fresh romaine lettuce, or by itself. Great served with meats for dinner, by itself for lunch, or as a delicious picnic dish.

Use a large salad bowl and toss in the following ingredients:

Peeled cucumbers cut to bite size

Quarter-cut vine-ripened tomatoes
(Costco has both of the former that are really good.)

Slice some white onion
(Walla Walla Sweets if you're in luck) or
Bermuda onions into rings and snap to manageable size

Cut a quarter cup of feta cheese into small cubes,
or crumble if preferred

Throw in a handful of Kalamata olives

Add thin slices of green, red, or yellow bell peppers

Drip some extra virgin olive oil and red wine vinegar
over this medley

Sprinkle liberally with oregano and black pepper

If the Feta is salty you won't need to salt

Tom Drougas moved to Sun Valley in 1975 while playing football in the NFL. As a first-round draft pick of the Baltimore Colts, the young tackle from the University of Oregon first blocked for Johnny Unitas, completing a five-year career in the pros playing two years for the Miami Dolphins. Raising a family in Ketchum has been the focus of the past 26 years. Tom's sons now work with him, and his wife, Cheri, offers healing hands to the community as an operating room nurse turned massage therapist.

Waking up the first morning after moving to Ketchum to the sound of five acres of sheep in front of my yard let me know we were in for a few surprises. Fortunately, I remember the smell of sagebrush in the springtime more than the sheep passing through!

SESAME BROCCOLI STIR-FRY SALAD

FROM MARIEL HEMINGWAY
IN MEMORY OF JACK HEMINGWAY (1923-2000)

Juice of 2 limes

2 tablespoons chopped fresh ginger + 1 teaspoon minced

2 cups broccoli florets

$1/4$ cup water

1 teaspoon cornstarch

$1/2$ teaspoon Asian sesame oil

4 garlic cloves, sliced

2 scallions, sliced

1 cup shiitake mushrooms, stemmed and finely sliced

1 red bell pepper, stemmed, seeded and cut julienne in 2-inch strips

$1/2$ carrot, cut into $1/2$-inch thick slices

1 cup low-sodium soy sauce

3 tablespoons mirin

2 tablespoons rice vinegar

4 cups shredded romaine lettuce

1 teaspoon black sesame seeds

© Paul Todd, Nature Conservancy

Serves 4.

Fill a large saucepan with water, add lime juice and chopped ginger and bring to a boil. Add broccoli and cook for about 50 seconds until the broccoli is bright green. Drain and rinse in cold water.

In a small bowl, whisk together the water and cornstarch until the cornstarch dissolves.

In a large sauté pan, heat sesame oil over medium heat. Add garlic, minced ginger, scallions, mushrooms, bell pepper and carrot. Stir-fry for 2 minutes until veggies begin to soften. Add soy sauce, mirin and vinegar. Stir-fry for 2 more minutes. Whisk again and then add the cornstarch mixture and simmer 30 seconds to thicken. Add broccoli and stir-fry for about 1 minute until heated through.

Divide lettuce among four plates and top with stir-fried veggies. Garnish with a pinch of sesame seeds and serve.

It's been said that Jack Hemingway was "the savior of Silver Creek." An avid fly fisherman who served Idaho as a Fish and Game commissioner in the 1970s, Jack spearheaded the effort to preserve Silver Creek and keep this legendary spring creek open to fly fishing only, with catch-and-release regulations. In a 1976 Nature Conservancy news article, Jack wrote: "There are red-winged blackbirds calling in the cattail marshes, geese clamoring on nesting sites, … bees are gathering pollen in the wildflowers, trout rising to early hatches, all mixed with the sound of the stream — the fishing regulars call it Silver Creek music."

Jack Hemingway was a composer, with his fly rod as his baton and nature as his orchestra. He was an enormous part of our community, and his good deeds remain a symphony for all of us to enjoy for years to come. Jack, your "music" will certainly be missed.

VAN'S TEXAS CHILI

FROM VAN WILLIAMS

This recipe is compliments of cinematographer John Stephens.

6 pounds hamburger

2 large cans stewed tomatoes

2 large cans chili beans

1 medium can garbanzo beans

3 bottles Chris and Pitts barbecue sauce

1 garlic, minced

1 can pitted black olives, chopped

4 large yellow onions, chopped

6-8 mushrooms, diced

2 tablespoons chili powder

1 bottle La Victoria salsa

2 cans corn

1 can diced chilies

$1/3$ box dark brown sugar (but I prefer to leave this out)

1 warm beer

Tabasco as desired

Sauté hamburger and transfer to a large pot. Add all other ingredients and combine well. Add beer to thin chili as desired. Simmer for 2+ hours, stirring often. Add Tabasco to spice it up, and serve.

Born and raised on a cattle ranch in Texas, Van Williams found his way to Hollywood in 1958. During the next twenty years he starred in several television series, but is best remembered as the star of *The Green Hornet*. In addition to his acting career, Van served with the L.A. County Sheriff's Department as a reserve deputy. After selling his communications company in southern California, he and his wife, Vicki, retired to the Wood River Valley. Van loves the changing seasons and the many recreational opportunities available here.

LISA MARIE'S BISON CHILI

FROM EDGAR BRONFMAN

14 pounds top round bison (you can order Georgetown Farm Bison from Buffalo Hill, 1-888-328.5326 or www.eatlean.com)

$9^1/_4$ pounds bottom round

2 bottles red wine (full body)

1 bunch celery

1 bunch carrots, roughly chopped

1 bunch flat-leaf parsley

6 Vidalia (sweet) onions

3 pounds white button mushrooms (sliced)

3 red, yellow and orange peppers (medium chopped)

4 tablespoons crushed garlic

6 tablespoons cumin

6 tablespoons chili powder

2 cans black beans

2 cans white beans

3 cans dark red beans

Flour for dredging seasoned with chili powder, cumin, onion and garlic powder, and paprika

Tabasco and chipotle peppers (depending on desired hotness)

Parmesan and Romano cheese (to taste)

Trim and cut meat into inch cubes. Sear trimmings and scraps in olive oil with 2 of the onions, carrots, celery and parsley. Cook for approximately 10 minutes in large pot. Fill with water and bring to boil. Reduce to approximately one-third, straining as needed. Meanwhile bring another very large pot, $^3/_4$ full of water with 1 bottle of red wine, to boil and let simmer. Dredge bison cubes in seasoned flour, sear and brown all sides in olive oil and place in simmering water. Continue until all meat is seared, deglazing with second bottle of red wine as needed. While both pots are reducing, sauté onions in olive oil until translucent, add garlic (do not burn), and cook for approximately 5 minutes. Add the chili and cumin powders, set aside. Sauté peppers. Set aside. Sauté mushrooms. Set aside. (It is important to sauté everything separately so it maintains its own flavor). Add "trimming" liquid (strained) to onion, garlic and spice mixture.

Bring to boil, then simmer to cook out chili and cumin flavor. Stir and cook until thick. Add peppers and mushrooms. Take off heat. Drain beans and rinse. Add to above. Meanwhile cook bison meat until tender. The mixture should be very thick and rich. The liquid should reduce to $^1/_2$ and heavily coat the bison. Take off stove. Add to mixture. Stir until well combined. Check seasonings, salt, Tabasco, chipotle peppers, Garnish with Parmesan and Romano cheese. Optional: Add 4 ounces dark semi-sweet chocolate. This amount of meat makes approximately 20 quarts.

Edgar M. Bronfman dedicated his career to The Seagram Company Ltd. He became president in 1971 and chairman in 1975. In 1994, he relinquished his position as CEO to his son, Edgar Bronfman, Jr., but continued to serve as chairman of the company until its merger into Vivendi Universal in 2000.

Mr. Bronfman is the president of the World Jewish Congress, an international federation of Jewish organizations whose goal is to preserve and foster the worldwide unity of Jewish people and to protect and nourish their heritage. Mr. Bronfman's many philanthropic and civic activities were recognized by President Clinton in 1999 when he was awarded the Presidential Medal of Freedom, the United States' highest civilian honor.

Edgar has seven children and twenty-one grandchildren. He and his wife, Jan Aronson, live in New York City, and spend their summers relaxing in Sun Valley.

DOG-GONE-GOOD SUN VALLEY CHILI

FROM RANDY ACKER

In a big pot, throw together:

2 cans chopped tomatoes

1 can kidney beans, slightly drained

1 can black beans, slightly drained

1 can butter beans, slightly drained

1 can chili beans, slightly drained

1 can red beans, slightly drained

1 can ranch-style beans, slightly drained

1 can garbanzo beans, slightly drained

Add any other color of beans you can find

1 can black olives, chopped

Add:

Sautéed hamburger, turkey or chicken (cut into cubes), as much or as little as desired

1 chopped onion

Lots of chopped garlic (or as much as your dog can stand!)

1 green pepper, chopped

1 red pepper, chopped

1 yellow pepper, chopped

Any other color of pepper you can find

Season with:

Brown sugar, to taste

Tons of chili powder

Salt & pepper to taste

Bring to boil, then simmer for one hour.

Serve with mozzarella and cheddar cheese sprinkled on top, or any other cheese you can find!

Top with Fritos. Enjoy! Howl at the moon!

Feeds a pack or a litter.

Randy Acker's life so far…

Randy has had his veterinary practice, Sun Valley Animal Center, for 21 years, and he's a favorite among dogs and owners alike. He also works on injured wildlife, and has rescued black bears, wolves, deer and a golden eagle.

He lives in Ketchum with his wife, Sue, their three kids, Amber, Maggie and Marcus, and his best friend, Labrador retriever Tate. His wife, Sue, continues to rescue abandoned kittens, so their bed is a little crowded! He enjoys skiing, biking, running, and camping, and when asked what it is about this valley that makes it home, he had this to say: "Go out on a trail early in the morning, look up at the trees and mountains, and you know why you live here."

NORTH FORK STEW

FROM ROD KAGAN

3 pounds beef chuck, cut into $\frac{1}{2}$-inch pieces

3 onions, diced

4 potatoes, peeled and cut into $\frac{1}{2}$-inch cubes

5 carrots, cut into 1-inch slices

1 package frozen string beans

Salt & pepper

Bay leaf

Garlic powder

Rosemary

In a big pot, cover beef with water and add desired amounts of salt, pepper, bay leaf, garlic powder and rosemary. Bring to a boil, then reduce heat, cover and simmer for 2 hours.

Stir in onions, potatoes and carrots, and simmer for another 30 minutes.

Just before serving, add frozen beans for a nice, green color. Reheat the next night for even better flavor!

Rod Kagan moved to Ketchum in the spring of 1973 and started building sculptures. In 1975 he built his home and studio in Chocolate Gulch and opened the first sculpture garden in Idaho. His many awards include a National Endowment for the Arts Fellowship Grant in 1984 and the Governor's Award for Excellence in 1990. Rod's other pleasures include skiing, hiking and fishing.

TURKISH STEW

FROM ANDREW & MICHELLE HARPER

2-2$\frac{1}{2}$ pounds lamb meat, cut into bite-size pieces

4 tablespoons margarine, diced

15 gibson onions (or frozen small white onions)

1 pound green beans

1 large eggplant

2 medium potatoes

2 medium carrots

4 large tomatoes

2 green peppers

2 pinches mixed herbs (preferably Herbes de Provençe)

1 dash garlic salt

Ground black pepper

$\frac{1}{2}$ tablespoon granulated sugar

$\frac{3}{4}$ glass of water

Slice the tomatoes into circles. Head, tail and string the beans and cut them in two. Scrape and cut the carrots lengthwise and cube them. After cutting the eggplant lengthwise in two, divide it from the middle and cube. Peel the onions. Remove the seeds of the green peppers and cut into pieces. Peel and cube the potatoes.

Put the cubed lamb meat into a big casserole dish, then layer with $\frac{1}{3}$ of the tomatoes, beans, carrots, eggplant and onions. Now add $\frac{1}{3}$ more of the tomatoes and all of the green peppers and potatoes. Top off with the remaining tomatoes. Add a dash of garlic salt, mixed herbs, pepper, sugar, margarine and water. Cover and place in a 350°F oven for 2-2$\frac{1}{2}$ hours. Remove from oven and serve hot with any of the great breads from Bigwood Bakery.

Since 1979, Andrew and Michelle Harper have published the quintessential guide for sophisticated travelers seeking out the world's most charming luxury hotels. Circling the globe incognito (Harper is a nom de plume), the peripatetic couple uncovers the most exclusive small retreats and then candidly shares their discoveries with other connoisseurs of the good life in the privately circulated Hideaway Report monthly newsletter. Between travels, they reside in Sun Valley (their "all-time favorite hideaway"). Their real name remains a well-kept secret among locals, who respect their privacy and need for confidentiality.

LAZY MAN'S CIOPPINO (SEAFOOD STEW)

FROM ANNIE WILLIAMS

Cioppino was started over 100 years ago, when Italian immigrants fished the Pacific coast. The combination of fish flavors and spicy tomato base creates a particularly pungent Mediterranean delight. I first tried this dish many years ago at Scoma's Restaurant in San Francisco's Fisherman's Wharf, and I have never tired of it. You can substitute or add mussels, clams, or any white fish (halibut or sole), cut into bite-size pieces. Experiment with your own creations!

$^1/_2$ onion, chopped

1 garlic clove, minced

1 teaspoon basil

1 bay leaf

Pinch of oregano

Pinch of sage

2 cans Italian stewed tomatoes

1 tablespoon tomato paste

Salt & pepper to taste

$^1/_4$ cup dry red wine

$1^1/_2$ pounds crabmeat, cooked

4 large oysters

8 scallops

8 prawns, shelled and deveined

Sauté onion and garlic in olive oil until soft. Add spices and allow to cook 5 more minutes. Add tomatoes, tomato paste, red wine, salt and pepper, and simmer at least 1 hour.

When ready to serve, add the seafood to the sauce and cook for about 5 minutes. Serve in bowls with plenty of sourdough French bread and a robust red wine.

Annie Williams first moved to Ketchum in the mid-'70s. An avid animal lover, she has been active with the Animal Shelter and is a local representative of Canine Companions for Independence, an organization that provides trained assistance dogs to persons with disabilities. Annie has raised seven puppies for the organization to date, and plans to keep on going.

With her love of the outdoors and a small community, and lots of wild and domestic animals, Sun Valley is the ideal place for Annie!

DIVERSITY STEW

FROM GREG CARR

As the name might imply, this dish is a "melting pot" concept. It should be tailored to your tastes, the season, and the dietary considerations of your guests. I recommend you read this recipe through completely before starting to cook. I would also get a little ahead on the chopping. Some can be done while you cook, but at least slice the garlic and dice the onions and the jalapeños. Dishes such as this have a tendency to grow, so start with a 16- or 20-quart soup pot. I always brown the ingredients well in a large cast iron skillet before adding them to the pot. That way, all the ingredients release their maximum natural flavors to the stew. The early stage of a stew is the only opportunity to concentrate the flavors. The more time you take at the beginning to carefully brown all the ingredients, the better your result will be.

8 (or more) cloves garlic, peeled

2 medium onions, diced

2 jalapeños, diced

4 ribs celery, diced

4 carrots, diced

2 red bell peppers, diced

2 small zucchini, seeded

1 large yam, peeled and diced $1/2$"

4 ears fresh corn, cut from the cob

1 pint small button mushrooms, split

2 boxes frozen, chopped spinach

$1/2$ pound smoked bacon

2 pounds chicken breast

1 pound bulk sausage (like Jimmy Dean)

3 16-ounce cans diced tomatoes

1 cup pinto beans

1 cup lentils

32 ounces chicken stock (preferably homemade)

2 tablespoons dark chili powder

Salt & freshly ground pepper

1 bunch fresh oregano

2 bunches cilantro

6 bay leaves

Cook beans and lentils in smaller pots with a bay leaf until soft, then season with a tablespoon of salt. Slice the bacon into thin strips and brown in the soup pot. As the bacon cooks, break the sausage into $1/4$" pieces and brown in the cast iron skillet. Slice the garlic lengthwise, and add to the bacon. Once the sausage is brown, add it to the soup pot. Season the chicken generously with salt and pepper, and brown well in the sausage fat. Set aside. Once the garlic is brown, add onions, pinch of salt, and chili powder and cook slowly until the onions are the color of a brown paper bag. Brown the carrots, celery, jalapeños, red peppers, zucchini, mushrooms and corn in small batches so each gets well browned. Add the yams without browning them. Add the tomatoes, beans, lentils and half the chicken stock to the pot and bring to a simmer. Add bay leaves and dry oregano. Add salt and pepper to taste during the cooking process. Simmer for 45 minutes, then check to ensure the yams are cooked. Adjust the consistency with chicken stock, if necessary, and finish by adding the chicken, spinach, and fresh oregano. Serve over jasmine rice with chopped, fresh oregano.

Greg Carr was the co-founder of Boston Technology, and later served as Chairman of Prodigy Internet. He established the Carr Center for Human Rights Policy at Harvard University, which supports research into the efficacy of governmental and non-governmental human rights efforts. He is currently supporting a five-year human rights campaign in northern Idaho. In 2000, Greg founded the Market Theater in Harvard Square and began renovating Harvard's former Pi Eta Club building to stage live performances. Greg is a part-time resident of the Wood River Valley, where he spends his summers and holidays.

LIGHTLY SPICED CORN CHOWDER WITH HOUSE-SMOKED SHRIMP

FROM CHEF BILL BRACKEN OF
THE BELEVEDERE AT THE PENINSULA BEVERLY HILLS

1/4 small onion, peeled & diced

1/2 celery stalk, diced

1/4 leek (white only),
cleaned & diced

2-3 slices jalapeño pepper, diced

1 shallot, diced

3 garlic cloves, crushed

1/2 pound sweet corn kernels

1 quart (1 litre) chicken stock

1 cup fresh cream

8 pieces shrimp,
medium size with shell

2 tablespoons sweet
corn kernels for garnish

Salt & pepper to taste

Serves 4.

Preparation time: 2 hours

Cooking/Set Up time: 5 minutes

Smoking Shrimp:

Drain and rinse the shrimp thoroughly. For smoking, any standard barbecue grill can be used. Fill the bottom pan of your barbecue with smoldering charcoal. Sprinkle about two inches of wood chips over the charcoal. Spray lightly with water to keep the wood chips moist. Keep the wood smoking. Lay the shrimp on the grill or rack and smile until completely cooked, turning halfway through. Peel the shell and slice the shrimps in half to garnish your soup.

In a medium-heat sauté pan, sauté the first ingredients until they are translucent. Do not brown. When the vegetables are almost cooked, add the corn kernels and chicken stock. Simmer on low heat to reduce the stock by half. Puree stock using a blender. Strain through a conical strainer with fine mesh. Return the stock to the sauté pan, bring to boiling point and season with a pinch of salt and white pepper. Serve in soup bowls and garnish with corn kernels and smoked shrimps.

Bill Bracken won a scholarship to the Culinary Institute of America through a national cooking competition in Kansas, his native state. He graduated with honors and went on to be voted the 1998 Chef of the Year by the California Restaurant Writers Association. Since he joined The Belvedere, the restaurant has been awarded the coveted AAA Five Diamond Award for six consecutive years and remains the only hotel restaurant in Southern California to win this award. Among his enticing signature dishes are Potato Crusted Chilean Sea Bass and Truffle Roasted Chateaubriand of Veal...almost as good as this chowder!

TOMATO CORN CHOWDER

FROM STARR WEEKES

Soup is my favorite culinary concoction. It's a meal in itself and can be as delicate as the softest spring breeze or as hearty and robust as chili or gumbo. The food prep doesn't require exact measurements, and it's a great way to get rid of leftovers. I think a soup should always be spontaneous. It's best to sauté veggies lightly in good quality olive oil and then add to the stock. I always purée approximately half of my overall pot in the blender to "thicken" my soups. A few cooked potatoes can be added to any soup for heartiness and to thicken. Do not be restricted by exact measurements.

In ½ cup olive oil, sauté in a big pot:

Celery, chopped

White onions, chopped

Green, red and yellow bell peppers, chopped

Garlic, minced or chopped

Scallion tops, chopped

Add:

1 can diced tomatoes

Water or half & half, depending on desirable thickness/thinness and quantity needed

At the very end, add frozen or fresh corn and spinach, cooked eggplant, meatballs, cheese, or anything you feel like adding.

Let it simmer, but never boil. Best served warm rather than hot!

Starr Weekes has spent a lifetime in food service, 30 years of that in Ketchum. She has served food at everything from week-long river trips to winter weddings in Wyoming, and has owned and operated two restaurants, cooked for cowboys in Mackay, hosted concessions at rodeos, bolted to Bend with wedding cakes, and cooked at backcountry yurts. And, with her children and grandchildren also in town, Starr puts on one big family spread. If you are ever lucky enough to sample Starr's cooking, most notably her soups, you will thank your lucky "Starrs!"

PASOLE

FROM LINDA PACKER

2 pounds of pork shoulder

$3^1/_2$ cups canned beef broth

3 cups water

2 medium onions, 1 sliced and 1 chopped

5 cloves garlic (or more if desired), 2 whole, 3 minced

$3/_4$ teaspoon oregano

Salt to taste

2 to 4 tablespoons GOOD New Mexico chili powder

2 to 4 cans white hominy, drained

3 medium tomatoes, chopped, or 1 28-ounce can whole tomatoes, drained and chopped

2 to 4 cans green chilies, chopped and drained

1 cup fresh coriander (optional)

In large pot, bring pork, beef broth, water, sliced onions, 2 whole garlic cloves and oregano to a boil over medium heat. Simmer for 2 to 3 hours, or until pork can be cubed. Reserve the meat and strain broth, discarding vegetables. Refrigerate broth until fat hardens, then skim.

In large pot, heat 1-2 tablespoons olive oil over medium heat. Add chopped onion and minced garlic and sauté until soft but not browned. Add cubed pork and chili powder, sauté a few minutes more, then add reserved pork broth, hominy, tomatoes, green chili and coriander. Adjust taste by adding more chili powder.

Simmer for another 45 minutes to one hour, so flavors will mix.

Serve posole with fresh sliced limes and tortillas.

A 4th generation Arizona native, Linda Packer spent part of her formative years on the Ft. Apache Indian reservation and in a small northern Arizona community not unlike Hailey. She moved to the Valley in 1990 and immediately became immersed in our community. As a member of the Board of Directors for the Sun Valley Center for the Arts, past President of the Board of Directors for the Sun Valley Center for the Arts and Chairman of the Board of Directors for Expedition Inspiration, Linda gives time and energy to the cultural enrichment of our community.

The mountains, the air and the never-ending vistas; the warm and friendly Wood River Valley community; the interesting people, the fun people and the caring people have kept Linda here to enjoy camping, hiking, bicycling, the galleries, the arts and the symphony.

LIGHTLY CURRIED AVOCADO GAZPACHO

FROM JEFF KEYS OF THE BELLEVUE BISTRO

I love soups, and this is one of my favorites. It's simple and delicious, so try it!

6 cups good chicken or vegetable stock

3-4 perfectly ripe avocados, peeled, seeded and sliced

1 medium white onion, diced

1 cucumber, peeled and sliced

$1/3$ cup freshly squeezed lime juice

$1^{1}/_{2}$ teaspoons curry powder

$1/3$ cup fresh snipped cilantro

A nice squirt of Tabasco or siracha

Salt & pepper to taste

Combine all ingredients in a large bowl, then coarsely purée small batches at a time in a food processor. Chill.

Serve soup with a dollop of pico de gallo and a drizzle of sour cream.

Jeff Keys was introduced to the food world in Aspen. He loved it, and began working with chefs around the world. In 1976, he opened his first restaurant. He has since opened five restaurants, including Soupçon in 1985, and The Bellevue Bistro in 1997.

Jeff and his wife, Sheila, together with their sons Austin, André and Ian, love the cultural opportunities and the close connection to nature that this valley offers.

TORTILLA SOUP

FROM KATE BERMAN

I finally put this recipe into writing for all the teachers at Hemingway School!

3 tablespoons butter, melted

4 tablespoons flour

1 onion, chopped finely

2 ribs celery, chopped finely

2 garlic cloves, chopped finely

49½-ounce can + 2 14½-ounce cans chicken broth

14½-ounce can diced tomatoes with juice

7-ounce can diced green chiles

¼ teaspoon crushed red pepper

½ teaspoon cumin

1 teaspoon chili powder

Juice from 1 lime

1 roasted red pepper, diced

Makes 2 quarts.

This valley would not be what it is today if it weren't people like Kate Berman who give unselfishly of their time and energy. Kate has made a career out of volunteering, primarily for the Hemingway School and the Sun Valley Ski Education Foundation. Thanks, Kate!

In a mediom, heavy soup pot on medium high heat, whisk butter and flour together, and stir until it's the color of peanut butter. Then add onion, celery and garlic. Continue to stir until the veggies are limp. Slowly whisk in chicken broth. Bring to a boil, then reduce heat to simmer and add tomatoes, green chiles, crushed red pepper, cumin, chili powder, lime and roasted red pepper. Simmer 1 hour and serve with garnishes.

Optional garnishes: cilantro, shredded jack cheese, shredded chicken, diced avocado, crisp broken unsalted tortilla chips.

NORTH CONWAY COUNTRY STEW

FROM TYLER PALMER

2 pounds lean beef stew meat, well trimmed and cut into 1-inch cubes

1 yellow onion, quartered

4 carrots, peeled and cut into 1-inch pieces

4 celery stalks, cut into 1-inch pieces

1 green bell pepper, seeded and cut into 1-inch pieces

$\frac{1}{4}$ cup quick-cooking tapioca

$\frac{1}{2}$ cup dry bread crumbs

1 pound whole mushrooms

1 $\frac{1}{4}$ teaspoon salt

$\frac{1}{4}$ teaspoon pepper

1 can (14 $\frac{1}{2}$ ounces) whole tomatoes, undrained and coarsely chopped

1 cup dry red wine

Preheat oven to 300°F. Combine all ingredients in a Dutch oven or 4-quart casserole dish, lightly coated with cooking spray or oil. Stir to mix well. Cover and bake for 4 hours.

Tyler Palmer was a member of the US Ski Team from 1968 to 1972, held the 3rd Overall World Cup Ski Title in 1971 and joined the US Olympic Team in 1972. From 1973 – 1978, Tyler was consistently the top American on the World Pro Skiing Tour. He's been coaching all levels of skiers ever since, and is currently coaching for the Sun Valley Ski Education Foundation.

Tyler continues to ski race on the Master's Circuit, astounding and pushing the limits of his competitors and himself. But when he takes time out from skiing, he enjoys to hunt and fish.

TURKEY CHILI

Ingredients:

2 cups diced onion

1 cup diced green bell peppers

$1/2$ cup diced green chilies

1 pound ground turkey

16-ounce can tomato sauce

16-ounce can diced tomatoes in juice

1 can pinto beans, drained

1 can kidney beans, drained

Sour cream

Cheddar cheese, shredded

Chili Spice:

2 tablespoons chili powder

2 tablespoons ground cumin

2 tablespoons oregano

1 tablespoon kosher salt

1 tablespoon garlic powder

1 tablespoon onion powder

$1/4$ teaspoon allspice

1 teaspoon cayenne

In a large pot, combine onion, bell peppers and green chilies and sauté in olive oil until translucent. Add chili spices and cook over low heat for 2 minutes, stirring continuously.

Add turkey and stir until cooked. Add tomato sauce, tomatoes and beans and cook for $1^{1}/_{2}$ hours. Serve with sour cream and cheddar cheese on top.

Alysia May grew up in Los Angeles persuing her passion for tennis. After 3 years playing on the WTA Professional Women's Tour, she opted to pursue her other passion, food, at the California Culinary School in San Francisco. Following stints at Auberge du Soleil in Napa Valley and The Belevedere at The Peninsula Hotel in Beverly Hills she relocated to Sun Valley and opened the Newslink Cafe.

Alysia sits on the board of Rachel's Network, a non-profit group that endeavors to place women in leadership positions of environmental organizations world-wide. She is also an active volunteer and supporter of The Advocates. She enjoys hiking with her dog, Mr. Peabody, and playing golf in this beautiful valley.

VENISON CHILI

FROM BUZZ ALDRIN

4 tablespoons butter

1 onion, chopped

4 cloves garlic, minced

4 tablespoons brown sugar

3 cups red wine

4 tablespoons balsamic vinegar

4 tablespoons tomato paste

4 tablespoons beef stock

1 teaspoon cumin

$\frac{1}{2}$ teaspoon cayenne pepper

$\frac{1}{2}$ teaspoon chili pepper

2 tablespoons cilantro, chopped

4 tablespoons olive oil

1 cup bacon, chopped

2 pounds venison meat, finely diced

2 cups canned black beans

Serves 6.

In a large pot over medium heat, melt butter and sauté onion and garlic until soft. Stir in brown sugar and cook until onions and garlic are light brown. Stir in red wine, vinegar, tomato paste and beef stock. Add cumin, cayenne pepper, chili powder, cilantro and salt. Bring to a boil, then simmer until reduced by half, about 30 minutes. Meanwhile, cook the bacon in a microwave oven or frying pan until brown and crunchy. Break into small pieces. Brown the venison in a frying pan and season with salt and pepper. Add the bacon and black beans and stir together. Transfer to the pot and combine with sauce. Simmer until the chili is thick, 20-40 minutes. Season to taste.

Buzz Aldrin has made it his lifelong mission to venture outward in space. His courageous missions include Apollo VIII, man's first flight around the moon, and the famous Apollo XI moon walk on July 20, 1969, when Buzz and Neil Armstrong became the first two humans to set foot on another world. The largest worldwide television audience in history witnessed that unprecedented heroic endeavor.

In 1993, Dr. Aldrin received a U.S. patent for a permanent space station he designed, and he later founded his rocket-design company, Starcraft Boosters, Inc.

Today, Dr. Aldrin remains at the forefront of efforts to ensure a continued leading role for America in manned space exploration. When he takes time out from his worldwide lectures, Buzz and his wife, Lois, explore the deep-sea world of scuba diving and ski the mountaintops of Sun Valley.

TOMATO SAUSAGE GUMBO

FROM MEL & MERILYN SCHWARTZ

This recipe is our modified version from The Diabetic Gourmet, *by Francine Prince. It represents a perfect partnership: Marilyn cooks this favorite of Mel's and he thoroughly enjoys eating it!*

1 bag frozen cut okra

1 tablespoon white vinegar

2 teaspoons olive oil

3 large cloves garlic, minced

2 teaspoons fresh ginger, peeled and shredded

1 medium onion, minced

2 tablespoons minced sweet green or red pepper

1 tablespoon wine vinegar

2 cans chicken broth

$1/2$ cup unsweetened apple juice

1 can diced tomatoes with liquid

1 tablespoon tomato paste

$1/2$ teaspoon crushed dried rosemary

$1/2$ teaspoon crushed dried thyme leaves

$1/2$ teaspoon fennel seed

$1/8$ teaspoon ground red pepper

2 tablespoons barley

2 bay leaves

2 chicken Thai sausages, cut up

Mel Schwartz won the Nobel Prize for Physics in 1988, and is Professor Emeritus from Columbia University in New York City. In 1995, he sold a computer security business that he founded.

Mel and Marilyn are now full-time residents in Sun Valley, after many winter ski trips since 1972.

Bring saucepan of water to boil. Add white vinegar and okra and boil for 2 minutes. Drain and set aside.

Heat oil and sauté garlic, ginger, onion and peppers over medium heat until lightly browned.

Add wine vinegar and cook for 30 seconds. Add remaining ingredients except the sausage and simmer for half an hour, stirring occasionally. Then add the sausage and cook another 15-20 minutes.

CHEESE BOOGIES

FROM LEN HARLIG

My wife and I have been vegetarians since 1966, long before cows became "mad" and carnivores "nervous." I created this meal, which can be served for breakfast or lunch. Don't mind your first instinct that these aren't breakfast fare flavors! Much better than bagels and lox, this recipe utilizes several food groups. The nutritional value is high, yet calories are moderate, depending on how much cheese is used. Enjoy!

English muffins

Grey Poupon mustard

Sweet pickle relish

Your favorite cheese

Sunflower seeds

Avocado, sliced thinly

Tomatoes, sliced thinly

Alfalfa sprouts

Split an English muffin and toast it lightly. Spread a thin coating of Grey Poupon mustard and sweet relish on the inside of the muffin.

Layer with your favorite cheese (I use sharp cheddar or Jarlsberg Swiss) and sprinkle with sunflower seeds. Toast in toaster oven or broil in oven until the cheese starts to melt. Remove and add avocado, tomatoes and sprouts.

Serve warm.

Len Harlig

Len Harlig and his wife, Carol, have been full-time residents of Blaine County for 25 years. Before coming here, Les was in the hospitality industry in Los Angeles. After spending several days in the Wood River Valley during a September visit in 1973, Carol and Len decided to move here, the most beautiful place they had ever found. To help preserve the environment and the quality of life in their new community, they became involved with numerous organizations. Len has since served eight years on the Blaine County Planning and Zoning Commission and was elected three times to the Blaine County Board of Commissioners. He recently retired from public office, but still serves on the Friedman Memorial Airport Authority, the Emergency Medical Service Council and the Criminal Justice Council. The Ketchum/Sun Valley Chamber of Commerce selected Len as Citizen of the Year 2000.

TOFU SANDWICH DELIGHT

FROM MARILYN MARTIN

This recipe tastes like tuna without the fishiness!

1 package firm or extra firm tofu, drained

3 tablespoons sweet relish

2 tablespoons Vegenaise or other eggless mayonnaise

2 tablespoons nutritional yeast

2 teaspoons mustard of choice

1 tablespoon tamari

2 celery stalks, chopped

A few drops vinegar

Salt & pepper to taste

Onion or green onion, sliced (optional)

Lettuce

Tomato, sliced

Avocado, sliced

Whole wheat bread

Mash tofu in a bowl (it's easiest with a potato masher). Add all remaining ingredients and mix thoroughly. Spread on whole wheat bread and top with lettuce, tomato and avocado. Mmmmmm!

The tofu mixture will easily last 5 days in the refrigerator.

Marilyn Martin started Idaho Animal Advocates in 1992, a local watchdog organization that is known for alerting the public to critical issues of animal abuse and exploitation by humans. She and her partner, Susan Rahmann, work to alleviate needless animal suffering in the Wood River Valley and all of Idaho. IAA believes that all animals deserve our respect and compassion.

Marilyn and has lived in Ketchum for over 15 years and enjoys nature and hiking with her rescued dogs.

Marilyn Martin

VEGGIES & SIDES

WILD RICE SALAD

FROM ROBERT & KATHRYN GARDNER OF GARDNER RANCHES

This recipe was shared with us by our dear friend Lucile, a niece of the Friedman (Airport) family. Enjoy!

1 cup wild rice, rinsed, cooked and cooled

$\frac{1}{3}$ cup olive oil

1 teaspoon salt

3 teaspoons red wine or sherry vinegar

$\frac{1}{2}$ cup scallions, diced

$\frac{1}{4}$ cup sweet red pepper, diced

$\frac{1}{4}$ cup green pepper, diced

$\frac{1}{4}$ cup parsley, roughly chopped

$\frac{1}{4}$ cup carrots, finely diced

$\frac{1}{2}$ cup orange sections, membranes removed (optional)

Makes 4 servings

Put the rice in a bowl and toss with the oil. Add salt, toss; add vinegar, toss. Add remaining ingredients, including the orange sections if desired. Toss well, checking for seasoning. Add freshly ground pepper to taste and serve.

SHE

Kathryn

Gardner Ranches grows alfalfa in addition to growing malting barley for Coors, and raising cattle. Robert and Kathryn's families have been in the ranching business in the Wood River Valley for three centuries, and four generations still live in Gannett and Hailey. "We know how lucky we are to reside in such a special community."

And if you've ever been lucky enough to fish from their property along the banks of Silver Creek, you've had a taste of heaven.

JOHN'S ASPARAGUS SALAD

FROM JOHN DEMETRE

Salad:

Butter lettuce

Asparagus, steamed

Bacon, cooked and crumbled

Feta cheese

Green and calamata olives

In a food processor or blender, blend together to make a sauce:

Red peppers that have been cleaned, baked and skinned

Shallots

Garlic

Roma tomatoes, seeded

Blend for 30 seconds, then add:

Olive oil

Fresh basil

Salt and pepper

Blend again.

Put 2-3 heaping tablespoons of sauce on a chilled plate. Add whole leaves of butter lettuce (I use 2-3 leaves, depending on the size). On top of the lettuce, add a generous portion of the asparagus. Top with bacon and crumbled feta cheese, and garnish with a couple of green and calamata olives off to the side.

John Demetre is an avid golfer and skier who has, since 1964, reveled in Sun Valley's beautiful light. It is here that he has designed his functional yet stylish athletic sportswear and ski clothing for his companies, Demetre and JD Sun Valley. John lives in the Valley with his wife, Sally, and has a wonderful son, Alec.

CAROL'S POTATOES

FROM KIRK ANDERSON

This recipe comes from my mother-in-law (slightly modified by my wife, Hillary), who makes these potatoes for me and my family. I hope you will enjoy this dish as much as I enjoy photographing Idaho's potatoes, which can be seen at my gallery at the Sun Valley-Friedman Memorial Airport.

10 small organic russet potatoes

Organic olive oil that sprays

8 ounces organic cheddar cheese

8 ounces raw, sharp organic cheddar cheese

Salt & pepper

$^1/_2$ cup organic milk

Serves 8-10.

Spray a covered Corningware casserole dish with olive oil. Slice the potatoes very thinly and place in cold water. Preheat oven to 375°F.

Grate the two cheeses and mix together. Drain the potatoes and pat dry. Layer as follows: potatoes, cheese, potatoes, salt & pepper, cheese, potatoes, cheese, and salt & pepper to top it off.

Pour $^1/_2$ cup organic milk over the potato layers, and bake for 45 minutes covered, then 45 minutes uncovered.

The Anderson family moved to Ketchum in the early 1970s and opened Chateau Drug. Kirk began photographing this beautiful area in 1974, and in 2000 released his book, *Idaho Discovered*, which captures the essence of his incredible journey throughout Idaho.

Along with photography and potatoes, Kirk's passions are golfing, mountain biking, skiing and gardening. He has an amazing garden surrounding his home north of Ketchum, where he lives with his wife, Hillary, and their three sons, Casey, James and Lukas.

Kirk is grateful for The Advocates and the many other organizations our area is fortunate to have, and enjoys helping them through his photography.

EGGPLANT STACK

FROM ARNOLD SCHWARZENEGGER

Eggplant (choose size for desired diameter of stack)

Roma tomatoes

Imported buffalo mozzarella

Extra virgin olive oil

Chopped garlic

Fresh basil

Arrugula

Salt

Balsamic dressing (your favorite)

Coarse black pepper

Cut eggplant into $1/2$-inch slices. Brush with olive oil, then dredge in garlic, and sprinkle with salt and pepper. Grill or cook under a broiler on one side only. Remove and let slices cool. Do not cook too much or the eggplant will become too soft. Slice Roma tomatoes about $1/4$-inch thick. Slice buffalo mozzarella $1/2$-inch thick (same as eggplant).

Layer eggplant (browned side up) and buffalo mozzarella. The cheese should be slightly inside the edge of the eggplant. Eggplant-cheese, eggplant-cheese, eggplant. Save the nicest slice for the top of the stack.

Arrange sliced Roma tomatoes on top, drizzle with olive oil, garlic, salt and black pepper. Cook stack under a broiler, not too close to the flame so the tomatoes brown only slightly just as the cheese starts to melt. Serve over a bed of arrugula dressed with balsamic dressing and garnish with fresh basil.

Arnold Schwarzenegger is certainly a name we won't soon forget. This bodybuilding champion has the biceps and the brains to take him a long way from his native home of Austria. His hunger for success in everything he undertakes has brought him to where he is today, ever since he crossed the ocean to the US to take part in the 1968 Mr. Universe competition. One of the most respected actors in Hollywood, Arnold is now in the comfortable position of being able to select the projects he wants to partake in. Sitting in the director's chair is also a potential goal in the near future for this man who made his American Dream come true.

Arnold is a familiar face in Sun Valley, whether he's on the slopes or in the weight room, but when his career calls and he must leave his home in the Valley, he says with a smile, "I'll be back!"

GRANDMA HARRISON'S PICKLES

FROM VERNA HARRAH

For a half-gallon jar:

Pickling cucumbers,
approximately 6-8 per jar

Pickling dill

Carrot & celery sticks

2 tablespoons plain salt

2 teaspoons pickling spices
(do not use too many red peppers!)

3 cloves chopped garlic

Pinch of alum

And, of course, a lot of love!

Sterilize jars and lids. Put head and stem of dill in the bottom of the jar, then a layer of cucumbers. Put 2 sticks each of carrots and celery between the cucumbers. Add salt and the rest of the ingredients. Add another head and stem of dill, another layer of cucumbers, carrots and celery. Fill jar with water to cover, follow directions on lids, seal and turn upside down until salt is dissolved. Store in a cool spot for 3 weeks. Then eat the best pickles you have ever had! Enjoy!

Verna Harrah became Co-Chairman of CL Cinema Line Films in 1992, and in 1994, took over the leadership of the company. Harrah has since bought out her partners and changed the name of her company to Middle Fork Productions. Harrah's company is currently in development on *Anaconda II* at Columbia Pictures and has several projects in various stages.

Verna was born in Nampa, Idaho, grew up in Twin Falls and resided in Sun Valley, where she owned two bookstores and founded a ski clothing company she named Peregrine.

Although she has moved to Los Angeles, Verna considers Sun Valley "home," feeling a deep connection with the beauty and tranquility of the area. To her, Idaho is the most beautiful place in the world.

TOMATO PIE

FROM CHAD SMITH

This is great on its own or served with a big salad.

1 9-inch piecrust

3 large, ripe, red tomatoes, cored, peeled and thickly sliced

$1/2$ teaspoon salt

$1/4$ teaspoon pepper

Fresh basil

$1/4$ cup chopped fresh chives

$1/4$ cup mayonnaise

1 cup shredded sharp cheddar cheese

Preheat oven to 425°. Bake crust for only 5 minutes. Reduce heat to 400°. Remove crust from oven. Line piecrust with tomato slices. Sprinkle with salt, pepper, basil and chives.

Mix mayonnaise and cheese thoroughly, then carefully spread evenly over the tomatoes, making sure to seal the edges of the piecrust completely. Bake for 35 minutes or until crust is brown and tomatoes bubbly.

Chad Smith grew up in the Wood River Valley and had his debut in acting on the stage of Wood River High School. He has appeared in Company of Fools' productions of *Side Man, A Christmas Carol, The Philadelphia Story, The Seagull, The Pied Piper* and *True West*, in which he co-starred with Bruce Willis. *True West* was also filmed for ShowTime. Chad is now counting his blessings and thanking his lucky stars. Who knows where we'll see him next!

CARROT SOUFFLÉ

FROM CHRISTINA HEALY

No family gathering would be complete without this recipe, given to me back in the 1980s by Lucy Lieder. I've added ginger to give it a little more zip! It's truly an elegant dish. Cooking, like designing a beautiful necklace, should be offered as a token of love, full of surprise and mystery. Enjoy!

2 cups cooked and puréed carrots
(can be done ahead of time— add lemon juice and cover)

2 teaspoons lemon juice

2 tablespoons minced onion

$\frac{1}{2}$ cup butter, softened

$\frac{1}{4}$ cup sugar

1 tablespoon flour

1 teaspoon salt

$\frac{1}{2}$ teaspoon cinnamon

1 cup milk

3 eggs

Grated fresh ginger (optional)

Beat all ingredients until smooth. Pour into a 2-quart, lightly buttered soufflé or casserole dish. Bake uncovered at 350°F for 45 minutes to an hour, until the center is firm to the touch.

Christina Healy

Christina Healy is a native Idahoan and has resided in the Wood River Valley since the 1970s. For over 25 years, her jewelry has been synonymous with the Sun Valley lifestyle. A friend of Christina's who collects her work in New York City once told her that she has the sophistication of a New Yorker with the heart of an Idahoan. What a compliment! Christina exhibits her work all over the U.S., but Idaho and the Wood River Valley will always be "home." Success may come in and out of her life, but her family and this community have always been here for Christina, and it's important to her to give back.

OVEN ROASTED VEGETABLES WITH GARLIC

FROM J.B. ROGERS

Here is one of my favorite vegetable dishes. My wife, Gwen, serves this with grilled flank steak and horseradish mashed potatoes.

6 parsnips, peeled, halved crosswise, then lengthwise

6 carrots, halved crosswise, then lengthwise

6 shallots, peeled, cut in half

2 medium-sized red onions, peeled, each cut into 8 wedges

1 large head garlic, separated into cloves, peeled

3 tablespoons chopped fresh rosemary or 1 tablespoon dried

3 tablespoons chopped fresh thyme or 1 tablespoon dried

2 tablespoons olive oil

2 tablespoons ($\frac{1}{4}$ stick) butter, melted

Salt & pepper to taste

Serves 6.

Preheat oven to 400°F. Mix first 7 ingredients in a large roasting pan. Drizzle with oil and butter and toss to coat. Roast vegetables until golden and tender, stirring occasionally, about 1 hour and 20 minutes. Season with salt and pepper. Transfer vegetables to a platter and serve.

Director J.B. Rogers directed the biggest summer comedy of 2001, *American Pie 2*. He made his directorial debut on *Say It Isn't So* after working with the Farrelly Brothers as Assistant Director/Co-Producer on *Dumb and Dumber, Kingpin, There's Something About Mary* and *Me, Myself & Irene*. His other credits include *3 Ninjas, Feeling Minnesota, Beverly Hills Ninja* and *American Pie*.

J.B. grew up in Indianapolis, and now lives in Sun Valley with his wife Gwen and two sons.

SWEET & SOUR ORZO AND VEGETABLE SALAD

FROM WILL CALDWELL

Quick, easy and delicious, this combination makes a refreshing first course or side dish with baked ham or deli sandwiches. Ideal for summer or winter!

Salad:

$1^1/_2$ cups orzo pasta

1 cup seeded, peeled cucumber, chopped

1 cup carrots, chopped

$^1/_2$ cup green onions or chives, chopped

1 green or red pepper, chopped

Lettuce leaves for garnish

Dressing:

$^1/_2$ cup white wine vinegar

2 tablespoons oil

3 tablespoons sugar

1 tablespoon fresh dill or 1 teaspoon dried dillweed

1 teaspoon salt

$^1/_4$ teaspoon ground red pepper

$^1/_4$ cup toasted sesame seeds

Serves 6.

Cook pasta until al dente, rinse with cold water, drain thoroughly, and refrigerate.

Prepare vegetables and dressing. Add to cold pasta and stir gently. Cover and refrigerate until serving time, up to one hour.

Line a serving bowl or individual salad plates with lettuce leaves and mound pasta salad on top. Sprinkle with sesame seeds.

Will Caldwell moved to the Valley from Oregon in 1971 and has since followed his passion as a fine art painter, exhibiting oils, pastels and prints in galleries locally and throughout the West. Primarily a painter of people, his diverse subject matter adorned The Advocates' first cookbook, and appears here again.

Will is an active part of our community as producer of the "Ketchum Alive" summer concert series, art teacher and exhibition organizer for young people's art, and co-founder of Idaho's leading forest conservation group, the Idaho Sporting Congress.

Will Caldwell

RUTH'S RICE & BROCCOLI CASSEROLE

FROM BUD & RUTH PURDY

$^3/_4$ cup finely chopped celery

$^3/_4$ cup finely chopped onion

1 package frozen chopped broccoli,
thawed in colander with hot water. Do not cook!

1 cup instant rice

1 can cream of mushroom soup

1 can cream of chicken soup

1 stick butter, melted

Cheez Whiz, melted

Preheat oven to 350°F. Combine all ingredients and blend well. Pour into a lightly greased casserole dish and bake for 20 minutes. Remove from oven, and reset oven to 210°F. Spread a layer of melted Cheez Whiz over the top and return to oven until cheese is bubbly, about 5-10 minutes.

You can also make ahead and refrigerate or freeze. When ready to serve, bake at 350°F for 30 minutes if cold, or 40 to 45 minutes if frozen. Continue with Cheez Whiz as above.

*Bud Purdy
+
Ruth Purdy*

Bud and Ruth Purdy's ranch is one of the oldest ranches in the Wood River Valley. The Picabo Livestock Co., also known as the Purdy Ranch, is over 115 years old! Bud's grandfather, W.H. Kilpatrick, and his two brothers homesteaded the original three sections in 1883. At that time, the Oregon Shortline Railroad was being built from Shoshone to Hailey.

Bud and Ruth bought the Kilpatrick Ranch from Bud's family in 1955 and have since added on to it. Today, they still farm about 4,000 acres and run several thousand head of cattle.

TOMATO CHUTNEY

FROM LYNN McCARTHY OF COTTONWOOD CATERING

This chutney is delicious served with flank steaks, chicken, lamb or pork.

2 cups sugar

3 cups cider vinegar

2 tablespoons fresh ginger root, peeled & minced

$2\frac{1}{2}$ teaspoons salt

$1\frac{1}{2}$ teaspoons coriander seeds, crushed lightly

$\frac{1}{2}$ teaspoon dried, red hot pepper flakes

3 pounds plum tomatoes, peeled, seeded & quartered

3 onions, chopped

1 cup golden raisins

In a large, heavy saucepan, combine sugar, vinegar, ginger root, salt, coriander seeds and red hot pepper flakes and bring to a boil, stirring until the sugar dissolves. Add the tomatoes, onions and raisins and simmer the mixture, stirring occasionally, for one hour, or until sauce is thickened. Let cool and transfer to a bowl or jars.

This chutney stays fresh for three weeks if kept covered and chilled or frozen. Makes about $3\frac{1}{2}$ cups.

Lynn McCarthy, chef and owner of The Cottonwood, has been cooking for over twenty years. She draws from her many cooking stints in San Francisco, France and Italy to create her wonderfully flavorful recipes. The Cottonwood offers catering and cooking classes with flare!

MEAT, GAME & POULTRY

BISON BRISKET

FROM JAN ARONSON

1 4-5-pound Bison Brisket
you can order Georgetown Farm Brisket from Buffalo Hill, 1-888-328-5326 or www.eatlean.com

2 large yellow onions, finely chopped

1 green bell pepper, finely chopped

1 red bell pepper, finely chopped

10 cloves garlic, finely chopped

2 large Portobella mushrooms, sliced thin and cut into $1/2$ inch pieces

Canola or other unsaturated oil

1 cup parsley, chopped

1 bottle dry red wine

1 large can Italian plum tomatoes, drained (save the liquid) and chopped

2 tablespoons rosemary

1 tablespoon thyme

1 tablespoon oregano

$1/2$ teaspoon cayenne pepper

Salt & pepper to taste

Serves 6-8.

Heat oil in a large wok or large, heavy pan and add onions, green and red peppers, and garlic. Sauté, stirring all the while, until ingredients are cooked but still firm. Add the mushrooms and cook until they are soft. Add chopped tomatoes and parsley, heat through. Add liquid from tomatoes, red wine, rosemary, thyme, oregano, freshly ground pepper and cayenne pepper. (This dish doesn't need much salt, as the flavors are very intense; but if you must, add salt sparingly!) Heat until the mixture is bubbling and very hot.

Wash the Brisket and remove any fat from the top. Bison is very lean and there will be very little fat to remove. Place the meat in a Dutch oven or large baking or roasting pan with a tightly fitting lid and pour the sauce over it, distributing the mixture evenly around the meat. Place the lid on the pan and cook in a preheated 325°F oven for 3 hours.

When done, carefully remove meat and slice across the grain into $1/2$-inch slices. Place sauce in a large bowl and serve with the meat.

Jan Aronson is a full-time artist whose talent has enriched the experience of students and spectators worldwide. Her work has been on exhibition at Winston Wachter Mayer Fine Arts in New York, United Nations in Geneva, The Discovery Museum in Bridgeport, Connecticut, and Ketchum's Anne Reed Gallery. Jan has created a balance of work and play, and she and her husband, Edgar Bronfman, have found Sun Valley to be the perfect place to spend their summers.

George's Cajun Meat Loaf

FROM GEORGE GREEN

I confess that I am still a junk food freak and eat all the wrong foods, but my wife, Wilma, is a vegetarian and eats only the right foods! Here is my latest recipe for my favorite meat loaf.

2 tablespoons
margarine or butter

2 medium carrots,
finely chopped

1 large onion, finely chopped

1 large celery stalk,
finely chopped

1 small green pepper,
finely chopped

2 garlic cloves, crushed

2 pounds ground meat
(veal, pork, and beef)

2 large eggs

1 cup fresh breadcrumbs

$1/4$ cup milk

1 tablespoon Worcestershire

2 teaspoons salt

1 teaspoon ground cumin

$1/2$ teaspoon black pepper

$1/2$ teaspoon dried thyme leaves

$1/2$ teaspoon ground nutmeg

$1/2$ teaspoon ground red pepper

$1/2$ cup + 2 tablespoons
ketchup

Garnish: fresh herbs

Prep: 20 minutes

Bake: 1 hour 15 minutes

Oven: 375°F

Serves 8.

In nonstick skillet, melt margarine or butter over medium heat. Add carrots, onion, celery, and green pepper, and cook until vegetables are tender (about 15 minutes), stirring occasionally. Add garlic and cook 1 minute longer. Set aside to cool slightly.

Preheat oven to 375°F. In large bowl, mix ground meat, eggs, breadcrumbs, milk, Worcestershire, salt, cumin, black pepper, thyme, nutmeg, ground red pepper, $1/2$ cup ketchup, and cooked vegetable mixture just until well combined but not overmixed.

In 13" by 9" metal baking pan, shape meat mixture into 10" by 5" loaf. Brush remaining 2 tablespoons ketchup over top of loaf. Bake meat loaf 1 hour and 15 minutes. Let stand 10 minutes before slicing. Garnish with herbs if you like.

George Green, president and CEO of Hearst Magazines International, is responsible for approximately 102 editions of Hearst Magazines in forty-two countries. Just a few of those include Cosmopolitan, Good Housekeeping, Redbook, Esquire, Harper's BAZAAR, Town & Country, House Beautiful, and O, The Oprah Magazine. In 1998, George received The Henry Johnson Fisher Award, the publishing community's highest accolade, and in 1999, he was the recipient of The ACE International Publishing Personality of the Year Award.

George and his wife, Wilma H. Jordan, president and chief operating officer of The Jordan, Edmiston Group, Inc., are delighted to be a part of this community, but regret that they and their children, Elizabeth and William, don't get more opportunities to enjoy Sun Valley and its many valued offerings.

BACHELOR'S DELIGHT

FROM PHIL PUCHNER

This recipe comes from school-time cooking at Colorado University. When I came back from Asia in 1968, I married a real cook, Ann, so I don't have to do this anymore. But it does give you a full meal!

Onions, chopped

Butter or oil

Ground beef

1 can spaghetti sauce

Brown onions in a skillet with butter (these days, you should probably use oil). Add crumbled ground beef. When it looks good and done, drop in a can of spaghetti sauce and stir. Heat until warm, then eat!

Phil Puchner, a ski-bum legend, came to Sun Valley in 1947 to pursue skiing and racing. He taught for Otto Long, John Litchfield and Sigi Engl, and raced in many Harriman Cups, placing third in a Downhill one year. Phil got his engineering degree during summer school so he could ski in the winters. He left in 1959 to work as an engineer in Asia and returned to the Valley in 1968. He quit downhill skiing in 1976 due to the poor snow that year, and he hasn't gotten back to it yet. But he is competing in the Masters Circuit in cross-country skiing, and although he claims it's his worst event since college, he manages to prevail every year in the Boulder Mountain Tour!

AFTER SHOW RIBS

FROM KIM MILLER FOR STEVE MILLER

This is a dish that I make for my husband, Steve Miller, and his bandmates for after the show. It has been a tradition for the last 14 years. Steve always asks me to tour with him and I'm flattered to be included with his life on the road. I'm a working girl and try to contribute however I can, taking photographs and cooking. The truck drivers put my barbeque in with the other equipment for the tour and sometimes I'll cook a leg of lamb or a turkey, but these ribs are the favorite. I also make a big Caesar salad to go along with the ribs.

2 pounds sauerkraut, fresh bags or 2 jars drained of juice

20 pork ribs, "country style," bone in

10 to 14 ounces K.C. Original Masterpiece B.B.Q. sauce or your favorite

Makes 10 servings of 2 ribs apiece.

My barbeque is a Weber, and I can fit an oval roasting pan inside it and close the lid. I put 20 briquettes on each side and use electric starts to light them.

Start your barbeque. Pre-heat Weber-style grill according to directions for cooking in the "indirect" method, as if you're baking: Place items to be cooked in a pan on the center part of the grill rack, between two evenly distributed piles of burning briquettes.

In a deep, heavy roasting pan or aluminum foil pan (2 if foil, for added support), place half of the sauerkraut. Layer your ribs over the sauerkraut. Add remaining sauerkraut on top of the ribs. Pour barbeque sauce over all ingredients.

Place uncovered pan in the center of your pre-heated grill, cover grill and cook for about 2 hours. You will need to add more briquettes after an hour; about 10 briquettes to each side of the pile works best. At the same time, take the ribs off the barbeque and stir them around to see how they're cooking. If you don't have a barbeque, you can cook the ribs in the oven at 325°F for about 2 hours. The ribs are done when they are separating from the bone.

Steve Miller

Steve Miller and his Blues Band debuted at San Francisco's Avalon Ballroom in 1967, with immediate success. Shortly after, the band signed with Capitol Records, and Steve demanded the most lucrative contract in music history, setting a new standard for future artists. Steve, along with his band and other great musicians, has since recorded and produced top albums such as *The Joker, Fly Like an Eagle, Book of Dreams* and *Abracadabra*. In 1993, Steve recorded *Wide River* at his studio north of Ketchum.

Continuing to sell over a million albums per year and performing at sold-out concerts throughout the U.S., The Steve Miller Band is still going strong. When they're not out on the road, Steve and his wife, Kim, reside in Ketchum.

BEST GRILLED SIRLOIN STEAK

FROM CONNIE PORTER

This is my family's favorite steak. Guests always love it, too. We usually serve it with a big green salad containing lots of fresh veggies. I have found that this will serve more people than one thinks because guests usually take only a few pieces. Leftovers are great served cold in sandwiches or salads. Enjoy!

1 piece of steak
Have the butcher cut you a 2-inch-thick (I mean it!) sirloin steak, boneless

1 package Good Seasons' Garlic and Cheese salad dressing mix - not the creamy kind - or some other oil and vinegar dressing to which you add crumbled blue cheese

1 package blue or Roquefort cheese

Prepare salad dressing mix per directions. Marinate meat in the dressing, refrigerated, for at least 24 hours. Turn meat several times so it is marinated thoroughly on both sides.

Remove from marinade and discard marinade. Grill meat to desired doneness. (I personally do not like well done.) Remove meat to cutting board and immediately spread some cheese on one side of meat while it is still hot. Let the meat rest for ten minutes.

To serve, cut diagonally across the grain in thin slices.

Connie Porter

During the Christmas holiday of 1979, Connie Porter first came to Sun Valley with her husband Dick, who had been coming here to ski since 1947. After the long drive from California, Connie stepped out of the car in Elkhorn and immediately felt at home. She loved the locale; but in a few days, she also fell in love with the people. Connie and Dick first bought a vacation condo, then moved here full time in 1987. They are both very involved in the community through supporting various charitable organizations, including St. Luke's Hospital Auxiliary. As much as they love the Valley, the most amazing assets to them are the wonderful people here. Connie spends most of her time volunteering, but she also enjoys horseback riding and gardening.

Bar Horseshoe Fajitas

FROM DAVID R. STOECKLEIN

2 pounds flank steak

$\frac{1}{2}$ cup vegetable oil

$\frac{1}{3}$ cup lime juice

2 packages Hidden Valley Original Ranch Salad Dressing Mix

1 teaspoon ground cumin

$\frac{1}{2}$ teaspoon black pepper

6 flour tortillas, warmed

Top with guacamole, sour cream and picante sauce

Serves 6.

Pierce steak all over with fork. Combine lime juice, oil, ranch mix, cumin, and pepper. Pour over steak, cover and refrigerate overnight.

Grill, using marinade to baste. Slice into thin slices and roll in tortillas with toppings. Enjoy!

Dave Stoecklein was born in Pittsburgh, and moved to Ketchum 22 years ago after living in Utah. He resides in Elkhorn with his wife, Mary; three sons, Drew, Taylor and Colby; dog, Maggie; cat, Scratcher, and the family's new pet, a climber badger they call Digger.

Dave has always loved Sun Valley. "It's a wonderful family town with a lot of great outdoor activities. After coming west 32 years ago to be a ski photographer, I continue my profession on the best ski mountain in the world."

SALTIMBOCCA (VEAL ROLLS)

Serve with tiny noodles, a crisp green salad, and chilled beer.

8 thin slices milk-fed veal

2 cups Parmesan cheese, grated

8 slices prosciutto ham

2 tablespoons brandy

4 tablespoons butter

4 tablespoons oil

1 clove garlic, crushed

$1/2$ teaspoon thyme

Salt and freshly ground pepper

1 tablespoon tomato paste

$1/2$ cup Marsala wine

2 tablespoons butter

$3/4$ cup beef broth

8 large mushroom caps

1 tablespoon lemon juice

2 tablespoons cornstarch

2 tablespoons parsley, chopped

Serves 8.

Prep time: about 40 minutes.

Place the thin veal slices on wax paper. Sprinkle the cheese over the meat and cover with wax paper. Pound the cheese well into the meat. Remove top wax paper and place a slice of prosciutto over the cheese. Brush on brandy and roll up carefully, securing with string. Place the butter and oil in a large skillet. When sizzling, brown the meat rolls on all sides. Remove the meat and add to the juices in skillet the garlic, thyme, salt and pepper, tomato paste, beef broth, and Marsala wine. When well mixed and bubbling, return the meat rolls. Reduce heat, cover skillet, and simmer for about 15 minutes. Meanwhile, melt 2 tablespoons of butter in another skillet and sauté the mushrooms over low heat. Now add the lemon juice to meat sauce and adjust seasoning. Mix the cornstarch with a little water and add gradually to the sauce. Stir constantly and add only enough of the cornstarch mixture to give the correct amount of thickening. Place the meat rolls on a hot platter and remove the strings. Pour the sauce around them and place a mushroom cap on top of each roll. Sprinkle parsley over all.

Myer Berlow is the former President of Worldwide Interactive Marketing for AOL and current President of Global Marketing Solutions for AOL Time Warner. He creates marketing solutions for advertising partners, focusing on transforming the way advertisers and marketers reach consumers. To date, Berlow has helped provide marketing solutions to nearly 20 partners, including eBay, Samsung, Bank of America, Wrangler, Nortel, Compaq, Qwest, Kinko's and Princess Cruises.

As America Online's President for Worldwide Interactive Marketing, Berlow oversaw account services, operations, and the #1 interactive marketing sales force in the industry. His sale force was named one of the top ten sales forces in the US by Sales and Marketing Management magazine.

Myer Berlow is a part-time resident of the Wood River Valley where he enjoys woodworking, fly fishing, and skiing.

TIM RYAN RIBS

FROM TIM RYAN

I stole this recipe more than forty years ago from an Ole Miss quarterback by the name of Jackie Parker, who starred for many years in the Canadian Football League. He was from Knoxville, Tennessee, but his Asian twist on barbecued ribs makes them the best "dry style" ribs I've ever had. And they're easy to prepare. Enjoy!

As many racks of fresh, baby-back pork ribs as you can handle. (But only baby-back ribs — they are leaner and meatier.)

Soy sauce

Lawry's Seasoned Salt (Use no substitutes!)

Liberally soak the racks in the soy sauce, marinating for about an hour before grilling. A few minutes before grilling, sprinkle a generous amount of Lawry's Seasoned Salt on both sides of the racks and rub in well.

Forget the nonsense about cooking pork low and slow. Ribs are thin, and cook best quickly over a high flame on your charcoal or gas grill.

When the grill is ready, start the ribs with the bony side down. Turn after 4 or 5 minutes. Repeat on the other side, tending carefully throughout. (A glass of wine for the chef during this process is permissible and, indeed, recommended.)

Remove the ribs when soy is slightly charred. With a hot fire, this should be no more than 15 minutes, probably less. Taste one rib to make sure you didn't screw up. For those who can't stand to be without it, spritz with freshly ground pepper.

Serve with Rhone red or Zinfandel, or if you must, a cold beer. Munch away!

Tim Ryan is a nationally known sports announcer who first came to Sun Valley in 1972. He has covered a variety of sports over a 42-year career — the last 30 with CBS and NBC, including NHL hockey, NFL and NCAA football, Grand Slam tennis, championship boxing and Olympic coverage of alpine skiing. Originally from Canada, Tim has since 1991 been a resident of Ketchum, where he loves skiing, tennis, hiking, good food and good people — but not necessarily in that order.

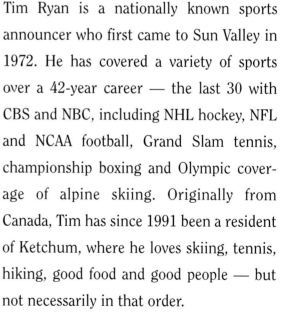

SIMPLE SAWTOOTH POT ROAST SUPREME

FROM ADAM WEST

Olive oil

Butter

1-2 cloves garlic, chopped

Onion, chopped

Salt & pepper

Pot roast cut of beef, elk, deer or moose

Potatoes, chopped

Carrots, chopped

Green, red and/or yellow peppers, chopped

Celery, chopped

Apple, chopped

Red pepper flakes

Dried apricots (optional)

Frozen green peas

Heat oven to 375°F.

In an old black iron skillet, pour a good dose of olive oil and smooth in a chunk of butter. Add garlic and onion and sauté.

Season the pot roast with salt and pepper. Braise meat on all sides in skillet. Place potatoes, carrots, peppers, celery, onions and apple around the meat. Salt a bit more and use a few red pepper flakes. Add hot water to mostly cover the roast. Cover pan with foil and place in oven and roast for about 4 hours, adding water when necessary. You might add a few pieces of dried apricot to the top of the roast. Ten minutes before done, pour frozen green peas over the top. Uncover and serve from the skillet.

Best known for his portrayal of Batman, Adam West has become a three-generation icon as one of few actors of this century with a LIFE Magazine cover, three of the most popular TV Guide covers and instant international first-name recognition. He has starred in five television series and over 40 feature films. His roles range from detective to doctor to cowboy to sociopath, and he continues to maintain a wide demographic as a guest on many television shows, including *Politically Incorrect, The Tonight Show* and *Conan*. Adam is also an animated star on The Simpsons and his voice has been heard on *Batman*, and Disney's *Redux Riding Hood*.

If you ever need a crime fighter, this Caped Crusader resides in Ketchum. You can look him up in the Names and Numbers telephone book, but good luck catching him!

Adam West

BABY BACK, BACK, BACK PORK RIBS

FROM CHRIS BERMAN

My brother's wife, Kate, is a fantastic cook and makes this, my favorite dish, when I visit Sun Valley.

6 pounds baby back pork ribs

1 can beer

Sauce

4 cups tomato ketchup (32-ounce bottle)

1 $^1\!/_3$ cups finely chopped onion

$^1\!/_4$ cup brown sugar

3 tablespoons lemon juice

3 tablespoons rum

3 tablespoons Worcestershire sauce

2 tablespoons Liquid Smoke

2 teaspoons Tabasco sauce

Serves 6.

Preheat oven to 350°F. Cut rib slabs in half, leaving 6-8 ribs per piece. Arrange ribs evenly in a large roasting pan, then add the beer. Cover pan very tightly with foil or lid to prevent steam from escaping. Bake for 3 hours, then drain and discard liquid.

Two hours into the baking time, combine all the sauce ingredients in a large saucepan. Simmer over low heat for 1 hour. Prepare your grill.

Cover ribs with sauce, reserving about 1$^1\!/_2$ cups for serving. Grill on barbecue for approximately 5 minutes per side, or until slightly charred. Serve at once with reserved sauce on the side.

In 1979, one month after its inception, ESPN hired a little-known 24-year-old sports anchor named Chris Berman. Over the next 21 years (and running), Berman has become one of America's most respected, popular, and in many ways most beloved sportscasters. He has been selected the National Sportscaster of the Year five times by his peers, and he and his various shows have won six Emmy Awards and 12 Cable ACEs.

Chris is famous for his witty use of nicknames while voicing over Major League Baseball highlights, and he takes the same humorous approach during visits to the Wood River Valley, whether producing a commercial for his brother Andy's sport shop, Paul Kenny's Ski and Sports, whitewater rafting the Salmon River, or sitting in the stands at the Days of the Old West Rodeo. Chris returns annually as a Ketchum celebrity in the Danny Thompson Memorial Golf Tournament, a benefit for local and national leukemia research.

LAMB AND RICE MEATBALLS

FROM SCOTT & ANNE MASON OF THE KETCHUM GRILL

3 $\frac{1}{3}$ pounds ground lamb

1 yellow onion, diced fine

1 cup wild rice ,cooked

1 egg

1 cup Japanese breadcrumbs

$\frac{2}{3}$ cup cream

$\frac{1}{3}$ cup milk

2 $\frac{2}{3}$ tablespoons herbes de Provence

1 $\frac{1}{3}$ tablespoons kosher salt

1 dash cayenne

1 cup tomato juice

Serves 10.

Preparation Time: 1:15

Mix milk, cream and breadcrumbs and allow to soak. Mix together with lamb, onion, rice, egg and seasonings. Shape into 2-ounce balls and brown in a hot skillet. Remove to baking pan, add tomato juice and bake, covered with lid or foil, for 40 minutes at 350°F. Serve with your favorite sauce.

A Valley resident for more than 13 years, Scott Mason has owned and operated the Ketchum Grill for the past 10. Apart from Scott's life as a chef, he is a past president of the Ketchum Sun Valley Rotary Club, President Elect of the Chamber of Commerce, and a passionate road bike rider. What attracted him most to the Wood River Valley was the affordable housing... but that was over 13 years ago!

Anne Mason came to the Valley as a new mother more than 13 years ago. As owner and pastry chef at the Ketchum Grill for the past 10 years, she has been featured in numerous national publications. An active school volunteer, Anne loves to hike with her two dogs and two children. Apart from following her husband here, Anne loves the fact that in Sun Valley children are allowed to grow up at a child's pace.

BEST DOG BONES IN EAST FORK

FROM SHEILA LIERMANN

I like my baby back pork ribs hot and sweet, but you can adjust the hot spices and sweet stuff to suit your taste. Our three dogs seem to like my combination of hot and sweet and, for once, they will wait patiently for the bones.

8 pounds baby back pork ribs, cut into 6-inch lengths

Marinade:

Garlic cloves, chopped, to taste

Ginger, chopped, to taste

1 onion, chopped

$\frac{1}{2}$ cup soy sauce

$\frac{1}{2}$ cup sherry or vermouth

$\frac{1}{3}$ cup rice vinegar

$\frac{1}{4}$ cup molasses

3 tablespoons hot chili oil

3 tablespoons olive oil

2 tablespoons ground ginger

Cayenne pepper to taste

Freshly ground
black pepper to taste

Sauce:

2 cups fruit preserves
(I usually use raspberry jam)

$\frac{1}{4}$ cup soy sauce

$\frac{1}{4}$ cup rice vinegar

2 tablespoons sesame oil

2 tablespoons hot mustard

2 tablespoons prepared
horseradish

Cayenne pepper to taste

Serves 6.

Sheila Liermann was expelled from home economics in high school, but that didn't stop her from pursuing her love of cooking. She produced the first *Sun Valley Celebrity & Local Heroes Cookbook* for The Advocates, and she co-authored *Famous Friends of the Wolf Cookbook* and the *Austin & Hill Country Celebrity Cookbook*. In 1998, she abandoned cooking to produce *Unconditional Love in Sun Valley*, a delightful collection of locals and their pets.

After graduating from the University of Montana in 1980, Sheila headed out of town with thirty bucks she borrowed from her brother. Ketchum was about as far as she could go, and she's been here ever since. Whenever she skis, she finishes the day on Olympic Ridge, looking out at the Pioneer Mountains with gratitude that she lives in a place filled with such natural beauty and fine people.

Mix the marinade ingredients together. Cut slits in the meat so the marinade can penetrate. Place the ribs and marinade in a plastic bag and, if you have time, marinate the ribs overnight. Preheat oven to 300°F. Line a large roasting pan with aluminum foil. Place the ribs in the pan, bone side up. (It's okay to layer the ribs.) Pour the marinade over the ribs and add enough water so ribs are covered. Cook ribs for 2 hours, turning once. Turn ribs bone side up again, cover the pan with foil, and cook for 1 additional hour.

Meanwhile, make the sauce. Combine sauce ingredients in a plastic bowl and microwave until just warmed through, about 45 seconds.

Remove cooked ribs from marinade and slather with sauce. You can either return the ribs to the oven and continue to bake at 300°F until they are good and sticky, about 20 minutes; or you can grill them for 8-10 minutes until they are glazed and brown.

MARINATED MESQUITE GRILLED RACK OF LAMB

FROM TOM NICKEL

Our menu continues to evolve over the years as we find and create delicious new ways to prepare a variety of foods. Our Mesquite Grilled Rack of Lamb, however, has been on our menu since they day we first opened in 1987. Longtime locals may remember Chef Tom Sanker, with whom I developed this marinade recipe in the kitchen of the infamous Creekside Restaurant. We think it's one of the best ones out there for lamb, and this continues to be one of our most popular entrees.

8 12-14-ounce French-cut racks of Spring Lamb

4 cups virgin olive oil

4 tablespoons rosemary *

4 tablespoons thyme *

4 tablespoons fresh chopped garlic

2 cups soy sauce

1 cup dry sherry

2 cups chopped green onions

2 cups good quality Merlot

*Dry rosemary and thyme work as well if not better than fresh!

With a clean towel, pat-dry any excess blood from the lamb. Set aside in a bowl or pan that will allow the racks to be completely submerged, except for the bare bones, when the marinade is poured over the top.

Combine all marinade ingredients and mix thoroughly. Some of the contents will tend to settle out, so whisk the mixture briskly just before pouring over the lamb. Pour the marinade over the lamb, making sure all the meat is completely submerged. Refrigerate, letting it marinate for about 5 hours.

Start your mesquite fire and let it burn down to a bed of hot coals. Standard charcoal briquettes will also work. Remove the lamb from the marinade, shaking off any excess liquid, and grill over your hot fire. Start with the fat side down, and allow about 4 minutes per side.

Remove from the grill and place in a shallow pan to finish off the cooking in a pre-heated 400°F oven. Somewhere between medium rare and medium is the best way to serve this lamb recipe.

Note: These can be cooked all the way through on the grill if you prefer, but be sure to turn them often enough to prevent charring.

With a sharp knife, cut about $3/4$ of the way through the rack between each bone just before serving.

Between the marinade and the mesquite wood, this lamb will have plenty of intense flavors as is, but we offer a simple mint sauce for those who wish.

2 ounces whole butter
1 teaspoon rosemary
8 ounces mint jelly
$3/4$ ounce Worcestershire sauce
Pinch of salt
Pinch of pepper

Combine in a saucepan over medium heat and whisk until all are blended thoroughly. Serve warm in a ramekin on the side.

Tom Nickel

SUCCULENT BARBEQUED LAMB RIBS

FROM JOHN & DIANE PEAVEY

This simple summertime favorite simmers in the oven for several hours before grilling, a step that makes the meat fork-tender while cooking away some of the fat. The final barbecue sauce is your choice. Experiment with anything you like, from Asian ginger to Mexican chipotle. Commercial barbecue sauces are fine, too. This popular main course can also be served as an appetizer; just ask the butcher to cut the ribs into 3-4-inch lengths.

Enough ribs to allow each person 4-6 apiece, or according to your own appetite.

One can/bottle of beer per each baking pan of ribs (does not need to be a fancy brew)

Garlic powder

Favorite homemade or bottled barbecue sauce

Place the ribs in a shallow baking dish. Pour beer over the meat, sprinkle generously with garlic powder, and cover pan with foil. Place in a slow 275°F oven for two to three hours.

After removing pan from oven, discard fatty liquid and cover ribs with your favorite bottled or homemade barbecue sauce. Place meat directly on a hot grill and brown on both sides. (This will not take long.)

Serve hot with several cold salads on the side, such as white bean with mint and feta cheese, and a ratatouille.

John Peavey

Diane Josephy Peavey

Lamb, of course. What else from former State Senator John Peavey, the third generation in his family to run sheep on Flat Top Sheep Company ranch, and his wife, Diane, a KBSU public radio storyteller? This is the family who urged the community to share the history and culture of the age-old profession that evolved into the annual October Trailing of the Sheep Festival.

Idaho lamb is the Peavey family's favorite food. It is raised naturally in the mountains and fed on wild grasses and plants that enhance an already almost perfect meat. There are many ways to cook lamb, but you cannot fail if you just use the basics – garlic, mint, and rosemary or thyme. Don't limit yourself to the traditional legs and chops; some of the most delicious cuts require taking a bit of risk, but the results are always worth it.

PECAN-CRUSTED PORK TENDERLOIN

This entrée has become an all-time favorite with both our restaurant customers and our catering clients.

Pecan-Crusted Pork

2 pork tenderloins, trimmed of any fat

3 eggs

1 cup milk

$1/4$ cup Dijon mustard

6 cups flour

4 cups pecans

$1/2$ cup fresh sage, leaves only

$1/2$-1 cup Japanese style breadcrumbs

Serves 4-6.

Bourbon Molasses Sauce

4 tablespoons minced shallots

2 cups good quality bourbon (Jim Beam)

2 cups molasses

$1/2$ cup quick brown gravy (recipe follows)

2 tablespoons cold butter, optional

Pork: Whisk together eggs, milk and Dijon in a large bowl and set aside. In food processor, grind pecans and sage until fine but not totally smooth. Transfer to a bowl. Add breadcrumbs to pecan mixture until the mixture just holds together when squeezed in your hand. To bread the pork, dredge in the flour, dip in the egg mixture, then lay in the pecan mixture and press the breading onto the pork firmly. In a large sauté pan, heat $1/4$ cup oil. Place pork in the pan and brown both sides. Pour off excess oil and place the pan in a 425°F oven for 10–12 minutes. Remove from the oven. Slice, sauce and enjoy!

Bourbon Molasses Sauce: Place shallots and bourbon in a saucepan and bring to a boil. Reduce liquid by half. (Bourbon is flammable and may ignite. Don't panic – you've just learned how to flambé!) Add molasses and gravy, reduce to a simmer, and whisk in butter. Season to taste with salt and pepper.

Quick Brown Gravy:

2 cups beef stock
2 tablespoons tomato paste
1 bay leaf
Pinch of oregano

2–3 tablespoons roux (melt 4 tablespoons butter, add 4–6 table spoons flour, whisk together over medium heat until mixture smells nutty)

Put everything except roux in saucepan, boil then reduce to a simmer. Add roux a little at a time and allow gravy to thicken. Simmer 15-20 minutes (adjust thickness by adding a little water or more roux).

Brian and Sue Ahern have been catering for Valley residents since 1990. You've no doubt tasted some of their wonderful creations at a wedding, dinner party, vintners' dinner or some other special event. Together they established the Full Moon Steakhouse, which opened in 1997 and provides guests a cozy atmosphere in which to enjoy flavor-rich foods and great wines. This special restaurant has become a favorite place for celebrations, a family night out or a romantic evening. Brian combines his extensive knowledge of nutrition with physical fitness by working as a personal trainer at the Sun Valley Athletic Club. Brian and Sue's favorite moments are spent with their son, Brogan.

PORK TENDERLOIN WITH RASPBERRY SAUCE

FROM MARC MAST

1 pound pork tenderloin

1 pound fresh raspberries

2 ounces fresh orange juice

$\frac{1}{3}$ cup teriyaki

4-6 cloves garlic

Blend raspberries with orange juice, teriyaki, and garlic. Strain to remove raspberry seeds, then reduce to remove excess liquid.

Barbecue the pork tenderloin until medium rare, slice the pork, cover with raspberry sauce, and enjoy this elegant yet simple dish.

sun valley adaptive sports

"If I can do this, I can do anything"

Marc Mast has been teaching adaptive skiing for 20 years. As a five-year member of Disabled Sports USA, National Clinic Team, he traveled around the country training ski instructors the special skills required to teach the disabled. In 1999, Mast was listed as one of the top 100 ski instructors in America by *Skiing Magazine*.

Some of Mast's students have gone on to win world cup and national championships, but his greatest joy comes from teaching those who thought that, due to their disability, they would never be able to ski — then watching them ski the bunny slopes and beyond.

In 1999, Marc Mast helped establish the Sun Valley Adaptive Sports Program, which is dedicated to enhancing the lives of people with disabilities through sports and recreation. Mast was attracted to Sun Valley by the myriad outdoor activities and the natural beauty.

CHICKEN AND CHERRIES JUBILEE

FROM STUART & RIVIAN GLICKMAN

This is a 3rd generation recipe from the family of Grandma Syril Glickman.

1 chicken broiler, cut into parts —
or chicken parts of your preference

1 bottle chili sauce

$1/_2$ cup brown sugar — more or less to taste

8-ounce can pitted dark cherries, with juice

8-ounce (approximately) jar of steamed
chestnuts — France makes VERY good chestnuts.

Salt and pepper the chicken. Broil skin-side up until chicken is crisp.
Mix chili sauce and sugar to taste. Pour and spread chili sauce mixture
over chicken. Cover tightly with silver paper (foil). Bake 1 hour at 350°F.
Remove foil; add cherries and juice and chestnuts. Bake 15 to 20
minutes, baste if necessary.

Ten years ago, Stuart and Rivian Glickman
came to Sun Valley for a visit and their
hearts were captured forever. They met very
special friends that brought yet more
treasures to their very happy lives.
Children, grandchildren, dogs, friends and
the serenity of Sun Valley — what more
could a person wish for?

Stuart has been in the television industry as
CEO of the Carsey-Werner Company,
producer of such celebrated shows as *A
Different World, Roseanne, and The Cosby
Show*. He is an entertainment attorney and
has been involved in many charities. Rivian
has embarked on so many adventures in
her life that she cannot find an accurate
word to characterize her many interesting
journeys, but it is her hope that her life will
continue in the same unpredictable way.

CHUNKY BARBEQUE CHICKEN

FROM PETER CETERA

1 can diced tomatoes, Italian seasoned

1 can tomato sauce

$1/2$ cup chopped onion

1 tablespoon brown sugar

1 tablespoon apple cider vinegar

1 tablespoon Worcestershire sauce

2 cloves garlic, crushed

$1/4$ teaspoon cayenne pepper

Salt & pepper

1 3-pound chicken, cut into sections (legs, breasts, etc.)

Serves 4.

Drain tomatoes and discard juice. Combine tomato sauce, onion, brown sugar, vinegar, Worcestershire sauce, garlic, cayenne pepper, salt and pepper in a saucepan and mix well.

Add drained tomatoes to saucepan and cook over medium heat, stirring occasionally until thickened, about 10-15 minutes.

Place chicken pieces on a platter and brush both sides with sauce, reserving 1 cup for later. Grill the chicken on a barbecue for about 40 minutes, turning over several times and brushing on more sauce with each flip. Serve hot off the grill.

Singer/songwriter Peter Cetera was born and raised in Chicago and has been a full-time Ketchum local since 1985. He can be seen enjoying our mountain trails, either on foot or on his mountain bike. Peter is a self-acclaimed "barbecue kind of guy," and this recipe is one of his favorites!

Peter Cetera

CASHEW CHICKEN

FROM JULIE MOSES OF ST. LUKE'S
WOOD RIVER MEDICAL CENTER AUXILIARY

This recipe came from Gee's East Wind in Springfield, Missouri, my hometown, where cashew chicken was supposedly "invented." I moved here when my husband, Jon, took the position of CEO of the Wood River Medical Center. We feel very fortunate to have been recruited here. We love the lifestyle, and like to ski, camp and golf, but never seem to find the time to actually do it all! I am currently serving as President-Elect of the Auxiliary.

2 pounds chicken breast cut into 1-inch chunks

4 eggs

1 cup milk

1 cup flour (or more)

Salt & pepper

Sauce

4 chicken bullion cubes

2 cups water

4 teaspoons oyster sauce

4 tablespoons cornstarch

2 tablespoons sugar

Toppings

1 can cashews

3 green onions, chopped

The St. Luke's Wood River Medical Center Auxiliary is a volunteer organization of over 400 members whose purpose is to raise funds to purchase medical equipment and fund services for the St. Luke's Wood River Medical Center. The Auxiliary was founded in 1958 as the Moritz Auxiliary. Since then, the Auxiliary has raised over $2.8 million that has gone to purchase major medical equipment for the hospital. Most recently, the Auxiliary gave over $200,000 to the Paramedic Program, and is currently working on raising funds for cardiac diagnostic equipment. For the past 30 years, the Auxiliary has wined and dined the valley with their major fundraiser, the annual Holiday Ball.

Mix flour, salt & pepper in a large bowl. Add chicken, stirring to coat, and let sit for 15 minutes. Mix eggs and milk. Take chicken from flour mixture and put in egg mixture. Let sit for 10 minutes. Roll chicken in flour and deep fry in a wok until golden.

Sauce: Bring water to a boil. Add bullion cubes, oyster sauce and sugar. Slowly stir in cornstarch. Cook until thickened.

Put chicken pieces on a platter. Pour sauce over chicken. Top with cashews and chopped green onion.

MOM'S CHICKEN CURRY

FROM MICHAEL & LESLIE ENGL

This recipe can also be used with beef, lamb, shellfish, tuna or a combination of vegetables.

$1/2$ cup butter

4 tablespoons chopped onions

2 cloves garlic, minced

4 tablespoons curry powder

6 tablespoons flour

8 chicken bouillon cubes

4 cups water

1 apple, pared and chopped

5-6 cups cooked chicken, cubed

1 pint vanilla soy milk

In melted butter, sauté onions and garlic with curry powder for 5 minutes. Add flour and stir until smooth. Combine bouillon and water and slowly add to flour mixture. Stir until thoroughly blended. Add apple and chicken and simmer, covered, for 1 hour. Add soy milk. Heat thoroughly without boiling.

Serve with fluffy white rice and 6-8 condiments from the following list:

Chopped bananas
Chutney
Grated hardboiled egg
Chopped green onions or chives
Coconut, shredded and toasted
Raisins
Chopped green pepper
Chopped peanuts
Chopped cucumbers

Michael Engl is the son of Peggy Emery Engl and Austrian Sigi Engl, who was one of Sun Valley's most popular ski instructors and ski school directors. The generosity of The Engl Trust has, over the years, helped to improve the quality of life in the Wood River Valley and Idaho through its grants to many organizations, including the Sun Valley Center for the Arts and Humanities and the Community Library. Leslie Engl is on the board of the Wolf Education and Research Center.

Their daughter Riley's wedding in 2000 to Timothy Mott, followed by the birth of their grandson, Jasper, in 2001, has brought great joy to the Engls.

Leslie A. Engl

VIRGINA'S CHICKEN AND DUMPLINGS

FROM HOLLY FOSTER-WELLS FOR PEGGY LEE

This recipe comes from my grandmother's chef, Virginia Bernard, and it's just delicious. It has been a family favorite for years. The recipe is surprisingly easy to make, but you would never know it by the taste. Virginia serves it with a green vegetable and a salad of cranberry sauce and Mandarin orange sections. Enjoy!

1 whole chicken, cut into pieces (leave the skin on for cooking)

3 cans of chicken broth

1 can cream of chicken soup

$1/4$ teaspoon salt

$1/2$ teaspoon pepper

$1/2$ teaspoon dried parsley flakes

2 tablespoons butter

2 cans refrigerated buttermilk biscuit dough

Wash the chicken and place in a Dutch oven. Add the chicken broth, salt, pepper, parsley flakes and butter. Bring the broth to a boil, cover and simmer for 1 hour. Add cream of chicken soup, and stir until blended. Simmer while you prepare the biscuits.

Open cans of buttermilk biscuits and separate them (they are precut). With kitchen shears, cut each biscuit into eight pieces. Do not over-handle dough, as it can become tough.

Bring broth to a rolling boil. Drop the biscuit pieces into the Dutch oven and gently stir them in so that they are submerged in the broth (do not over-stir). Keep the rolling boil going for five minutes, then turn off the heat and cover. Let sit covered for 20 minutes. If you desire, remove the skin from the chicken before serving.

Holly Foster-Wells considers herself blessed to have grown up in Ketchum and still calls it "home" to this day. She currently lives in Studio City, California, and has managed the business of her grandmother, Peggy Lee, for the last two years. Singer Peggy Lee has touched generations with her angelic voice in classic Disney films like *Lady and the Tramp*. Prior to that, Holly worked for a number of years in television production design on such shows as *Seinfeld, Will & Grace, Third Rock from the Sun, Roseanne,* and *The Cosby Show*. While on a trip home to the Valley in 1996, Holly re-met an old Wood River High School friend, Dan Wells. The two were married in 1998 and had their first child in October 2001. Holly and Dan visit their family and friends in the Wood River Valley as frequently as possible.

Holly Foster Wells

CHICKEN AND PEANUTS

FROM JIM HOLCOMB

I've made this dish for 26 years and it has never failed!

3 chicken breasts, skinned and boned

4 scallions (or one small onion)

2 cloves garlic (or $^1/_4$ teaspoon powered garlic)

2 one-inch cubes fresh ginger (or $^1/_4$ teaspoon ground ginger)

6 tablespoons soy sauce (or tamari sauce)

4 teaspoons cornstarch

4 tablespoons water

2 tablespoons molasses

$^1/_2$ teaspoon cayenne pepper

3-6 tablespoons vegetable oil

$^1/_2$ cup peanuts

Serves 4.

Cut chicken into 1- to 2-inch pieces.

Dice up scallions, white part and green stalks.

Mince garlic and chop ginger.

In a separate bowl, combine soy sauce, cornstarch, water, molasses and pepper, and set aside.

Heat 2 tablespoons oil in frying pan or wok; add chicken and stir-fry until it loses its pinkness.

Add 1 tablespoon oil and add scallions, garlic and ginger; quickly stir-fry until lightly browned.

Add molasses and cornstarch mixture, and finally peanuts. Stir for 1-2 minutes.

Serve over rice.

Jim made us promise not to lose his photo, saying he will never catch another fish like this one!

Jim Holcomb's handpainted sinks and tiles adorn many homes, ranches and restaurants with images of wildlife, wildflowers, trout, and the graceful flies that fish feed on. For 21 years, he has run Idaho Mudworks, handpainting sinks, tiles and pottery that reflect the icons of our Valley. Jim was also a backcountry ranger for the Forest Service until he became a fly-fishing guide with Silver Creek Outfitters, and a talented and revered one at that. Just ask anyone that he has hosted on saltwater fishing trips to the Christmas Islands. With Jim, you are sure to catch your dream fish!

J. Holcomb

BRENTINA'S PAN-AMERICAN GOLD CHICKEN

FROM RIVER GROVE FARM

4 halved boneless, skinless chicken breasts

2 Mexican beers

1 large can Las Palmas green enchilada sauce

1 large can diced green chilies

1 pound pepper jack cheese, grated

1 cup shelled pistachio nuts

Serves 4.

Preheat oven to 350°F.

Open both beers. Poach chicken breasts in one beer until cooked thoroughly. It's okay if breast is browned. Begin drinking other beer.

After chicken is cooked, remove from pan. Slice chicken into bite-size strips. Place in baking dish. Drink some more beer. Pour green enchilada sauce over chicken strips. Evenly place diced green chilies over chicken and sauce. Spread grated cheese on top of everything. Cover and bake for 30 minutes or until bubbling. Remove cover, sprinkle pistachios on top. Bake 10 more minutes. Finish beer.

Serve with warm flour tortillas and condiments of choice.
We recommend:
Cilantro
Lettuce
Guacamole
Sour Cream
Diced green onions
. . . and more beer!

River Grove Farm is a horse-training facility located one mile north of Hailey, in a park-like setting on the Wood River. Bob and Debbie McDonald manage the farm and train the horses. Debbie McDonald is considered one of the top Dressage riders in the United States. Riding River Grove Farm's mare "Brentina," Debbie won two gold medals representing the United States at the 1999 Pan-American Games. Debbie and Brentina more recently won the 2001 National Grand Prix Championship in Gladstone, New Jersey. Brentina and Debbie are major contenders internationally, representing the United States.

CHICKEN CACCIATORA

FROM CARL MANUS A.K.A. GRANDPA SHRED

This recipe is loosely based on one I got from Mother Leone's cookbook. She started the world-famous Leone's Restaurant in NYC in the early 1900s. Since I do about 90 percent of the cooking these days at our home, I have fine-tuned this recipe over the years and it is one of my favorites. I hope it will become one of yours, too.

1 chicken, cut up

2 tablespoons olive oil

1-2 ounces salt pork, diced

2 tablespoons butter

1 large onion, diced

Chicken livers and gizzards, finely chopped

1 large garlic clove, mashed

1 teaspoon fresh rosemary

5-6 sprigs Italian parsley, leaves only

1 15-ounce can tomatoes

1 15-ounce can tomato sauce

1 6-ounce can tomato paste

$1/2$ cup dry red wine

Salt & pepper to taste

Spaghetti noodles

Combine oil, salt pork and butter in large pot. Add onions, chicken pieces, liver and gizzards. Brown (about 10 minutes). Chop rosemary and parsley, mix with garlic, and add to the pot. Stir and cook 5 minutes. Add tomatoes, sauce, paste and wine. Simmer about 30 minutes or until done. Add salt & pepper. Do not overcook! (Note: if you like a thicker sauce, add one more can of tomato paste.) Serve with spaghetti, spooning sauce over all. It would be a shame to serve this without a bottle of good, dry red wine.

Carl Manus, fondly called "Grandpa Shred" by young and old alike, moved to Sun Valley in January 1974 as a direct result of the energy crisis. He thought he'd hang out here 'til things settled down for a year or two, then head back to the So Cal rat race. Well, 27 years later, he's still here. Still "hangin' out" and lovin' it. "Best move I ever made!"

This area has everything Carl needs. He snowboards almost every day in the winter, and the rest of the year, he enjoys golf, fly fishing and mountain biking in these picture-postcard surroundings. What's not to love about that? On a crystal-clear powder day, you can hear Carl's delight echo through the runs on Baldy as he hoots, "DY-NO-MITE!"

CREPES HELENE

FROM BILL STOVER

Begin with a basic crepe batter (recipe below), add your favorite spices and herbs to taste. Basil, oregano, tarragon, parsley, thyme, chives, alone or in combination add incredible flavor to this entrée.

Basic Crepe Batter:

4 eggs beaten

2 cups milk

2 tablespoons soft or melted butter

2 cups all-purpose, pre-sifted flour

$1/2$ teaspoon salt

Herbs as desired

Crepes Helene:

2 cups fresh mushrooms, sliced

4 tablespoons butter

4 cups chicken, cooked and cubed

1 teaspoon salt

1 cup mayonnaise

$1/4$ cup sherry

1 cup sour cream

$1/2$ cup almonds, slivered, sliced or roughly diced

1 bunch seedless green grapes

2 bell peppers seeded and sliced in $1/4$-inch complete rounds (best to use 1 each of green, red, yellow or orange to provide color for garnish)

1 pound asparagus, steamed to firmly tender

Crepes: In a mixing bowl, add milk to beaten eggs. Gradually add flour, whisking constantly until smooth. Mixture should be the consistency of heavy cream. Fold in herbs, cover tightly and refrigerate for at least one hour. If batter is too thick, add 1 – 2 tablespoons milk. After refrigeration, use either a crepe or greased omelet pan to form crepes. Heat pan to medium heat and add about $1/2$ cup of mixture to pan, swirl evenly across the bottom of pan to form a round, thin crepe. Remove from pan when top surface of crepe has lost its gloss. Stack crepes until ready to fill.

Filling: Sauté mushrooms in butter. When mushrooms are golden, add chicken and salt, and fold together. Place mushrooms and chicken in a large bowl and set aside. In a separate bowl, mix mayonnaise, sherry and sour cream. Combine half of mayonnaise mixture with mushrooms and chicken. Fill crepes and roll tightly. Place filled crepes on non-stick, spray-coated cookie sheet, and spoon remaining mayonnaise mixture across tops of rolled crepes. Sprinkle with almonds. Pre-heat oven to 300°F and bake crepes for 20 – 30 minutes or until tops are slightly golden. Remove from oven, place on individual plates, and garnish.

Garnish: Center two bell pepper rings on top of crepes, insert two steamed asparagus stalks through center of double ring to form a V inside an O and scatter 4 or 5 grapes around dish.

Bill Stover's passion for corporate finance, exotic cars and his lovely wife Laura represent this gentleman's commitment to life. As Vice President of Finance and CFO of Micron Technology, Inc., Bill has guided Micron through the turbulent financial waters of the semiconducto industry since 1994.

The Stover family has found their Sun Valley retreat to be a wonderful way in which to enjoy time together in the unique atmosphere of the Wood River community.

KB's Burritos

FROM JOHN BURKE

Flour tortilla

Your favorite cheese, grated

Mexican rice

Refried beans

Guacamole

Chicken, cooked and chopped or shredded

Salsa

In a skillet, melt cheese on a tortilla. Add rice, beans, guacamole, chicken and salsa. Roll it up and enjoy!

John Burke moved to Sun Valley in 1975. He played hockey for the Sun Valley Suns for 12 years, and coached the team for 8 years. He was managing Paul Kenny's when golf pro Charlie Bolling Jr. came into the shop. John kiddingly told him that if he ever needed a caddie, he should give him a call. Three weeks later, Charlie called! John's rookie experience as caddie helped Charlie lose his tour card but, luckily for John, Charlie's friendship with Brad Faxon led to a 12-year career as Brad's caddie. Now in his second year as caddie for Davis Love III, John is on the road 27 weeks a year. When he goes on vacation, he comes home to Sun Valley. "There is just no better place on earth to come home to. Sun Valley has the best people, the best aesthetics, and the best quality of life." And when John comes home, he looks forward to his favorite KB's burrito.

John R. Burke

PAN-ROASTED PHEASANT WITH PEPPER COMPOTE

FROM PHEASANTS FOREVER

$1/4$ cup olive oil

1 large sweet red onion, thinly sliced

1 red bell pepper, thinly sliced

1 yellow bell pepper, thinly sliced

2 tablespoons butter

2 shallots, finely chopped

2 large white mushroom, finely chopped

1 cup pheasant or chicken broth

$1/2$ cup dry white wine

$1/2$ cup heavy cream

$1^{1}/_{2}$ tablespoons Dijon mustard

1 tablespoon chopped fresh tarragon

4 pheasants, breasted, skinless

Salt and pepper

8 tablespoons pesto

In a skillet, heat 2 tablespoons of the oil. Add the onion and bell peppers and cook over moderate heat until the onion is translucent, about five minutes. Transfer to a plate and keep warm.

In the same skillet combine the shallots, butter and mushrooms and cook over moderately high heat until browned. Add the broth and wine and cook until reduced by half, about six minutes. Add the cream and mustard and cook until slightly thickened. Strain the sauce through a coarse sieve. Stir in the tarragon, season with salt and pepper to taste, and keep warm.

In a large skillet, heat the remaining two tablespoons of oil over high heat, season the pheasant with salt and pepper and cook until the inside of the meat is just pink.

Place the onion/pepper compote on warm plates. Spoon the mustard sauce around the compote, place the pheasant on top, and drizzle the pesto over the pheasant breasts.

Pheasants Forever is a national conservation organization with more than 90,000 members. Locally, it's stronger than ever, with an annual banquet held each fall.

CURRIED GAME HENS

Sauces make the world go 'round! I don't like spending too much time cooking when there are so many other things to do, but I love good food. This recipe is very easy, very fast and very good!

2 game hens (20 ounces) defrosted*

1¹/₂-2 tablespoons curry powder**

2 tablespoons soy sauce

¹/₂ cup mustard

¹/₂ cup honey

Optional: raisins, sliced onions, sliced mushrooms

Serves 2 big appetites or 4 smaller ones.

*You can use regular chicken in this recipe, too.

**Curry powder is a mixture of many spices and varies by brand. Like some other spices and most herbs, it can lose its potency with age. Shelf life is about 6 months. I like using a combination of sweet curry and hot curry in this recipe.

Preheat oven to 350°F. Combine the above ingredients, including the optional ones, and place in a casserole dish. Place the game hens in the dish and marinate for 10-15 minutes, turning frequently. Cover with foil and bake for 30 minutes, then flip the hens over, remove the foil and bake another 30 minutes or until done.

Serve with couscous and colorful vegetables. This sauce is great on the couscous!!!

Muffy Ritz has lived in Ketchum since 1990. Being an avid adventurer, she's rarely in the kitchen, but loves to cook. You might find her riding her bike across the country, teaching her VAMPS (women's nordic ski clinics), coaching the ski team kids, doing the Eco-Challenge, climbing mountains, playing with her friends, or making chocolate chip cookies.

APRICOT-GLAZED GAME BIRDS WITH WILD RICE PILAF FROM CLINT STENNET

This delicious glaze is perfect for Cornish game hens, chicken, and game birds with light meat such as pheasant, partridge and quail.

Apricot Glaze:

1 12-ounce jar apricot preserves

$1/2$ cup Grand Marnier

$1/2$ stick (4 tablespoons) butter

$1/4$ cup orange juice

Birds:

4 Cornish hens or quail, 2 chickens or pheasants or 3 partridges

Wild Rice Pilaf:
A nice prepackaged wild rice blend or pilaf with herbs is easiest. (Prepare as directed on package first if you are stuffing the birds.)

OR

$1/2$ cup cooked wild rice

1 cup cooked basmati, brown, or white rice

Water or unsalted chicken broth (see note below*)

2 tablespoons butter

$1/2$ cup slivered or sliced almonds

2 garlic cloves, chopped

Herbs to taste (thyme, parsley, chives, savory, sage)

Salt and pepper to taste

*Rice varieties cook differently, so cook the wild rice separately from the other rice that you choose, following instructions on the package. Cooking wild rice with salt extends cooking time, so add salt after cooking. If the rice pilaf is a side dish, prepare it while the birds are cooking. If you stuff the birds, prepare the rice pilaf first. Drizzle some glaze on top of the rice side dish.

Glaze:
In a saucepan, over medium heat, whisk all glaze ingredients together and cook until thickened a bit, but be careful not to burn. Set aside.

Birds:
Wash thawed birds under cold water, then lightly salt and butter them. Stuff the birds with rice pilaf if you choose. Coat birds with some of the glaze. For Cornish hens and chicken, bake in a greased pan, uncovered. For game birds, bake in chicken stock in a covered pan, browning the top for only a few minutes at the end. Bake in 375°F oven for 45 minutes to 1 hour. Baste with glaze frequently throughout the baking period.

Rice:
Lightly sauté the butter, almonds, and garlic, then blend together with the cooked rice. Add the herbs, salt, and pepper to taste.

Clint Stennett is in his 11th year in the Idaho State Legislature, where he serves as the Senate Minority Leader. The former owner of the Wood River Journal & KSKI-FM, he currently owns and operates Ketchum/Sun Valley Television. He also owns and operates a cattle ranch near Mackay. He and his wife, Michelle, love chasing fish and game and spending as much time as possible in all outdoor pursuits under the beautiful Idaho sky. Clint can be spotted wearing a giant grin during the brown drake hatch on Silver Creek.

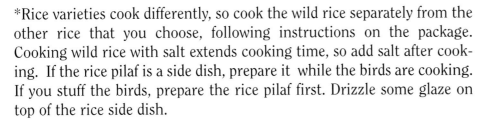

DEL FUEGO RICE & UPLAND GAME

FROM TERRY RING OF SILVERCREEK OUTFITTERS

Suitable for any white meat upland game or even chicken, this recipe is reminiscent of paella but is less costly, easier to prepare and more succulent. Just the thing for a cold winter night, the warm moist rice seems to have a tonic effect on a cold body and provide moral protection from the storm.

3 tablespoons olive oil

1 medium onion, finely chopped

$1^1/_2$ cups long-grain rice

1 bottle dry white wine

The breast meat of two pheasants or four chukars, or the breast on bone of six quail: Bone and cut the meat (except for quail) into bite-size pieces

1 package Lipton's onion soup mix

$^3/_4$ can of Campbell's cream of mushroom soup

10 ounces frozen peas, thawed

4 Basque chorizos, chopped into 1-inch lengths

3 tablespoons domestic curry

1 tablespoon Lea & Perrins Worcestershire sauce

1 tablespoon chopped garlic

Serves 6.

In a large skillet, sauté the chopped onion in the olive oil over a medium flame.

When the onion begins to become clear, add the rice, onion soup mix and cream of mushroom soup, along with two Campbell's cans of tap water. Cook on a medium fire, always adding water in order to maintain a liquid mixture.

Conscientiously test the rice by removing a few grains with a spoon. About the time the rice becomes nutty (can be chewed but is not cooked) add the chorizos, meat, Lea & Perrins, curry and garlic. Continue to keep the mixture runny, but now with the white wine.

When the rice is done, add the peas and slowly cook out the remaining liquid.

Terry Ring and his Silver Creek Outfitters offer exciting fishing adventures and clinics, opening up the world of fly fishing to locals and visitors alike. Terry's photography reflects the beauty that resonates when one is out casting to a fanciful trout.

PAN-SEARED DUCK BREAST

FROM CHEF RODRIGO HERRERA AT THE VALLEY CLUB

5 pounds boneless duck breast (skin on)

2 tablespoons olive oil

Salt & pepper

Orange Brandy and Dried Craisin Sauce:

1 tablespoon chopped garlic

2 tablespoons chopped shallots

$^3/_4$ cup dried craisins

1 cup brandy

$^1/_2$ cup orange juice (preferably fresh-squeezed)

$^1/_2$ tablespoon orange zest, finely chopped

$1^1/_4$ cups demi glaze

1 tablespoon chopped parsley

$1^1/_2$ ounces cold butter

Salt & pepper to taste

Serves 8.

Trim all extra fat from duck breasts, season them with salt and pepper and set aside.

Put oil in a pan and place on flame until it becomes smoking hot, then place duck breasts in the pan, skin-side down, until golden brown. Pull them off the heat and set them on a sheet pan, skin-side up. Put them into a 500°F oven for 8 minutes for medium rare, 10 minutes for medium, or 11 minutes for medium well.

Drain all fat from the pan, add garlic, shallots and dried craisins and brown for one minute, then deglaze the pan with brandy. Reduce to half and add the orange juice, demi glaze and orange zest, and reduce to desired consistency. Swirl in the butter and adjust the seasoning with salt and pepper. Finish it off with chopped parsley. Drizzle sauce over each duck breast.

THE VALLEY CLUB

Opened in 1996, The Valley Club is the only private Country Club in Sun Valley. The Valley Club offers all the amenities expected from the finest clubs in the world including a Championship 18 hole, Hale Irwin designed golf course, pool and tennis facilities and a full service clubhouse offering cuisine from the casual to the exquisite.

LESLIE'S PHAMOUS PHEASANT PHILLETS

FROM DR. MAURICE HORNOCKER

This is my wife, Leslie's recipe, and it's my favorite pheasant treatment.

1 pound pheasant breast fillets

1 egg

1 cup milk

Italian-style breadcrumbs

Parmesan cheese, grated

Whisk egg and milk and set aside. Mix breadcrumbs and Parmesan and place on a flat dish or plate; set aside.

Place the pheasant fillets between 2 sheets of waxed paper and, using a meat mallet smooth-side down, thin the fillets like veal cutlets.

Dredge in egg and milk mixture, then coat in breadcrumbs and cheese.

Heat olive oil in a skillet and brown fillets on both sides. Turn heat to low and cover for 5 minutes. Don't overcook!

Maurice Hornocker is a wildlife biologist best known for his research on the world's big cats. In his 35-year career, he and his colleagues have conducted pioneering research in North America on cougar, lynx, bobcat and ocelot; on leopards in Africa and Far-Eastern Asia; jaguars in Central and South America; and tigers in India and Siberia. Dr. Hornocker has also done groundbreaking research on other carnivores in North America: bears, wolverines, river otters and badgers. He is Director of the Hornocker Wildlife Institute, a nonprofit research and education foundation he founded in 1985.

Dr. Hornocker first visited Sun Valley in 1968 and fell in love with the area. He and his wife, Leslie, made annual skiing visits over the years before moving here in 1988. They love everything about the Wood River Valley — the skiing, weather, mix of people and all the outdoor opportunities. He and Leslie and their horses and dogs live on a small farm near Sun Valley.

LUKE'S DUCK

FROM LUKE WHALEN

This recipe, which I prepared for my cooking show, is fool proof. Enjoy!

4 tablespoons olive oil

$1/2$ cup dry white wine

6 tablespoons teriyaki sauce

$1^1/_2$ tablespoons cracked black pepper

4 mallard duck breasts without skin or bone

Place oil, wine and teriyaki into skillet and sprinkle the bottom of the skillet with one tablespoon of cracked black pepper. Heat on medium high until hot. Add breasts and cook for seven minutes. Turn breasts, sprinkle the remaining pepper on them, add a dash of teriyaki sauce to each and cook for six more minutes.

Remove the breasts and set aside (the meat should be red on the inside). Reduce sauce until slightly thickened. Slice the duck breasts thinly on a bias. Place duck on serving plate and spoon sauce over the meat. If you have guests who are squeamish about meat that runs red, stir the sliced duck into the hot sauce quickly before placing on the serving dish.

Luke Whalen is a vibrant character in our community. He has been a family dentist in Hailey since 1976 and, as an avid hunter and fisherman, taught the glorious techniques of delicious wild game cooking on his show, *The Wild Gourmet*, on channel 13 in the 1980s. Luke is a member of the national board of directors of Pheasants Forever, a national conservation group dedicated to providing habitat for wild animals.

BONELESS DUCK BREAST WITH APRICOT MUSTARD SAUCE

FROM LES &
LESLIE DILLEY

With Les and their four kids, Leslie has learned to take shortcuts as much as possible when preparing traditionally long-winded meals. Duck is one of Les's favorites, and when Leslie can find it frozen and boneless on the grocer's shelf, she knows she can make quick work of it with this recipe. The sauce can be prepared while the duck is in the broiler. This duck goes very well with a side dish of wild rice and oven-roasted asparagus. Enjoy!

Prep duck breast by pulling fat away from meat, leaving the fat still attached, but just barely. The fat will cut away easily when the duck is cooked, but will add flavor while broiling. Sprinkle on freshly cracked pepper to taste. Broil duck breast about 7 minutes on each side. Remove fat and slice thinly.

Quick Apricot Mustard Sauce

2 tablespoons dry white sherry

2 tablespoons apricot preserves
(smooth or chunky — try to get one without a lot of sugar)

1 tablespoon mustard

Heat sherry in a sauté pan on medium heat. Mix preserves and mustard together and add to pre-heated sherry. Stir and reduce for several minutes.

Top sliced duck with a tablespoon or two of sauce to taste.

Leslie Dilley, a Welshman, was born in the Rhondda Valley, Wales, in the United Kingdom in 1941 and moved to Los Angeles in 1986. Les has worked in the film business since 1956. As an art director, his credits include *Star Wars, Superman, Alien, The Empire Strikes Back* and *Raiders of the Lost Ark*. Dilley's work as production designer includes *Alien, Legend, The Abyss, Guilty by Suspicion, Casper, How To Make an American Quilt, Diabolique, The Peacemaker, Deep Impact*, and most recently *Pay It Forward, Men of Honor, and Black Knight*. Dilley has earned five Academy Award nominations, and has won two Academy Awards for Best Art Director for *Raiders of the Lost Ark* and *Star Wars*. He has also acted in some of the films he has designed, including *Pay It Forward, Deep Impact, Peacemaker*, and *The Distinguished Gentleman*.

Les and his wife, Leslie, were looking for a rural area in which to raise their four children, with one prerequisite: a nearby ice rink so Les could play his favorite sport: ice hockey. So, in 1994, they packed up and moved to Sun Valley.

ELK STROGANOFF

FROM FRANK & SUE ROWLAND

This recipe has been a family favorite in Elk Camp for years. It always brings good luck!

1 tablespoon flour

$^{1}/_{2}$ teaspoon salt (optional)

1 pound elk sirloin, cut in $^{1}/_{4}$-inch strips*

2 tablespoons flour

1 cup fresh mushrooms, thinly sliced

$^{1}/_{2}$ cup chopped onion

4 or 5 cloves garlic, minced

4 tablespoons butter

3 tablespoons flour

6-ounce can tomato paste

3 teaspoons kitchen bouquet

1 can beef broth

1 cup sour cream

3 tablespoons dry white wine

*If you have a piece of elk that is not a tender cut, marinate it in the refrigerator overnight in $^{1}/_{2}$ cup olive oil, $^{1}/_{4}$ cup wine vinegar, $^{1}/_{2}$ cup chopped onion, salt, 2 teaspoons Worcestershire sauce and minced garlic. Stir several times while marinating.

Combine 1 tablespoon flour and salt; dredge meat in mixture. Heat skillet to medium high and add 2 tablespoons butter. When melted, add sirloin strips and brown quickly, turning to brown all sides. Add mushrooms, onion, and garlic; cook until onion is tender.

Remove meat, onion and mushrooms from pan; set aside. Add 2 tablespoons butter to pan drippings and melt. Blend in 3 tablespoons flour, then add tomato paste and kitchen bouquet; blend, then add beef broth and cook slowly, stirring constantly until mixture thickens. Return meat and mushrooms to pan and simmer until meat is tender (about 30 minutes). Just before serving, add the sour cream and white wine, mix well and heat briefly.

Serve with wild rice, parsleyed and buttered noodles or your favorite pasta, candlelight and a fine red wine. This is even tastier when prepared a day before serving.

"Mrs. Sue"

Frank Rowland

Frank and Sue Rowland moved to Blaine County in 1972 when Frank was hired by the SNRA, and later by Power Engineers. Sue skied Baldy as a child, and Frank spent his summers in the Sawtooth Valley as a little tyke with his Forest Ranger father, so they jumped at the chance to move here. Things were a lot different in 1972. Hailey was a sleepy little town, and the Rowlands' children often asked why the doorbell never rang! But it didn't take long for them to become immersed in the community. Frank dedicated 16 years to the Blaine County School Board; Sue opened Sue's Pre-School, which for 28 years broadened the hearts and minds of so many children. "Mrs. Sue," as she is affectionately known, is a legend among kids and grownups alike.

Through the years, Sue and Frank have given every spare moment to help make our community flourish. When they aren't skiing Baldy's heavenly slopes or backpacking into Frank's secret spots, they are helping out at Blaine Manor Auxiliary, Expedition Inspiration, Canine Companions or as courtesy patrol on the Harriman Trail.

FISH & SEAFOOD

WARM SPRINGS PAN-FRIED TROUT

FROM CHEF MIKE OVERSBY AT
WARM SPRINGS RANCH RESTAURANT

2 6-12-ounce rainbow trout, boned

1 cup buttermilk

1 cup flour

1 teaspoon salt

2 teaspoons lemon pepper

1 teaspoon granulated garlic

1 cup cooking oil

Lemon wedges

Parsley

Soak trout in buttermilk for 30 minutes. Drain. Mix flour, lemon pepper and garlic. Dredge trout in flour mixture and refrigerate for one hour.

In a 12-inch sauté pan, heat oil to 365°F and fry both sides of the trout until golden brown. Top with fresh parsley and lemon wedges.

Originally named Warm Springs Ranch Inn, the former potato farm was purchased by Owen Simpson in the late 1940s and converted to a horse and cattle ranch. Private fishponds were established, making it a picturesque site for the restaurant that was built in 1953. Patrons could catch their dinner from the well-stocked trout ponds. The present-day tennis club was the site of the local rodeo grounds in the '50s. In 1960 the golf course was completed, and Jack and Mary Lou Simpson further enlarged the restaurant and bar. This uniquely scenic property, owned by the Simpson family, and the traditional Western American-style food and warm company has made Warm Springs Ranch Restaurant a favorite for many years.

IDAHO TROUT

FROM IDAHO'S FIRST LADY PATRICIA KEMPTHORNE

2-3 tablespoons butter

4 trout, heads and tails intact

Salt and pepper to taste

Lemon wedges

Topping:

1 shallot, finely chopped

$1/2$ pound mushrooms, finely chopped

2 tablespoons butter

3 parsley sprigs

Salt and pepper to taste

Serves 4.

Patricia Kempthorne, married to Idaho Governor Dirk Kempthorne since 1977, grew up in Boise, Idaho, and graduated from the University of Idaho with a degree in business management. The First Lady's interests encompass issues concerning children, families and communities, and finding solutions to the specific challenges they face, including parenting, education, healthy life choices and work-life balance.

The Governor and First Lady Kempthorne have two children, Heather and Jeff. They enjoy spending time as a family in the beautiful Idaho community of Sun Valley, fishing, golfing and relaxing. With its unique hospitality and flavor for Idaho's history, particularly that of the Hemingway legacy, they both feel welcome in Sun Valley and look forward to time spent here.

Rinse and dry the fish thoroughly. Cut 4 ovals of baking parchment or brown wrapping paper large enough to enclose the fish. Generously spread butter in center of oval. Place fish in center and sprinkle with salt and pepper; include cavity. Spread topping on the fish and fold paper over it, folding the edges over twice. (Moisten edges with beaten egg if brown paper is used.) Place on a baking sheet and bake at 350°F for 15 to 18 minutes. Garnish with lemon wedges and top with mushroom and onion topping.

Topping: Chop shallot very fine. Add mushrooms chopped very fine. In a heavy saucepan, melt butter and add mushroom and onion mixture. Cook for 3 to 5 minutes over medium-high heat. Stir until all of the moisture has evaporated. Remove from heat. Add chopped parsley and season with salt and pepper. (Not suitable for freezing.)

Marinated Copper River Salmon

FROM MARJOE GORTNER

Serve with a nicely chilled Sancerre. Bon appetit!

Half a side of Copper River Salmon
(available mid-May to June)

1 box of #9 spaghetti cooked al dente

Marinade :

1 small jar of mayonnaise

1 onion, chopped

6 cloves garlic, minced

Juice of 3 lemons

Serves 6.

Sauce:

6 cloves garlic, minced

$1/4$ teaspoon crushed red chili peppers (optional for an additional kick)

6 tablespoons extra virgin olive oil

Marinade: Mix all ingredients well. Place salmon in a flat dish and coat both sides with marinade. Leave in the refrigerator for 3 to 6 hours.

Create 2 "boats" out of aluminum foil large enough to hold the salmon.

Pre-heat outdoor grill on high for 15 minutes. Transfer salmon skin-side down onto the first aluminum-foil boat and place on grill. Close grill cover and cook on high for 8-10 minutes. Turn salmon over skin-side up onto second foil boat and cook 3 minutes more.

Serve with garlic spaghetti.

Sauce: Heat oil in a pan and add garlic and chili peppers. Blanch for 30-45 seconds (garlic should not brown). Add pasta and toss lightly. Garnish with parsley and arrange on plates with sliced salmon.

GARDEN STEELHEAD

FROM JASON ROTH OF IDAHO STEELHEAD AND SALMON UNLIMITED

Fresh steelhead or
salmon fillets (skin on)

1 red or white onion,
thinly sliced

1 green onion, chopped

Brown crimini
mushrooms, quartered

Red pepper, sliced lengthwise

Asparagus spears, medium size

1 lemon, sliced
into thin wheels

Fresh sprigs of dill

Capers

Mayonnaise or Miracle Whip

Lemon and herb vinaigrette,
or substitute your favorite

Butter, optional

White pepper and salt

*Chinook Salmon Daily Bag Limit; Clearwater River,
May 13, 2000*

Start with heavy-duty aluminum foil. Place two sheets down and overlap for a double layer where fillets will lie, leaving enough to gather and seal at the top and sides. Spray foil with Pam, then glaze with a light coating of mayonnaise and vinaigrette. Place fish, skin-side down, on foil and season with salt and white pepper. Glaze flesh lightly with mayonnaise and vinaigrette. Arrange small lumps of butter, capers, dill and lemon on top of fish. Finish preparation by arranging mushrooms, red pepper, onion and asparagus atop and beside fish.

Gather foil at the top and sides to seal and place on a grill over medium to medium-high fire. Check fish at about 10 minutes, depending on the size of the fillets. Promptly remove from grill and serve just after the thickest portion of fillet flakes with a fork.

Since 1984, Idaho Steelhead and Salmon Unlimited has been a leading voice on behalf of protecting steelhead and salmon resources and related economies. Formed by a diverse group of business leaders, guides, conservationists, sport fishermen and concerned citizens, ISSU and its 3,000 members are committed to the restoration of healthy populations of anadromous fish. ISSU is a scientific, educational and charitable organization incorporated under federal and state non-profit laws. Thanks to the involvement of locals such as Jason Roth, the Wood River Chapter of the ISSU is gaining tremendous momentum.

Fool-Proof Salmon in a Bag

FROM REX CHANDLER

During an Alaskan salmon fishing trip, a crusty old guide taught Rex Chandler this universally adaptable recipe, which can be prepared on camping trips or picnics over an open campfire or on the barbecue at home. The combination of baking and steaming is the key. The sealed foil pouch keeps the salmon moist and delicate. It's great for entertaining because it can be left on the fire without worry of over-charring. Set it on the picnic table, open the foil, and enjoy; or, for an elegant presentation, serve on a large platter with garnish.

1 side of salmon, about 5-6 pounds, bones removed and skin left on

1 orange, sliced into wheels

1 lime, sliced into wheels

1 lemon, sliced into wheels

$1/4$ cup chopped cilantro

$1/4$ cup chopped dill

$1/4$ cup white wine

$1/4$ cup extra virgin olive oil

Sea salt

Aluminum foil

Place salmon skin-side down, centered on several layers of foil, overlapping the foil loosely. Arrange citrus slices over the top of the salmon. Sprinkle chopped herbs on top of citrus. Pour white wine and oil on top. Sprinkle with sea salt. Place additional foil over the top and crimp the edges together to create an airtight cooking pouch or bag. Bake, roast, or barbecue until salmon is cooked to your liking!

REX CHANDLER

Rex Chandler learned the love of cooking from his mother and has been a restaurateur all of his life. After refining his skills in Hawaii, Chandler returned home to Newport Beach, California, where he created The Rex of Newport, recognized by the Restaurant Writers Guild as the finest seafood restaurant in Southern California for ten consecutive years. Looking to retire from the big-city environment, he relocated to the Wood River Valley and opened Chandler's Restaurant in 1994. Chandler's prides itself as the "Locals' Home of Fine Dining," specializing in seafood, prime meats and game.

Our great community atmosphere, with its wonderful schools, healthy environment and wide range of outdoor activities, is just the place for Rex to raise his young son. Aside from managing Chandler's, he is also president of the Sun Valley Restaurant Association.

JACK DANIELS SALMON

FROM JANE WOOSTER SCOTT

$^1/_2$ cup packed light brown sugar

2 tablespoons bourbon (preferably Jack Daniels)

1 tablespoon Dijon-style mustard

1 teaspoon soy sauce

$^1/_4$ teaspoon coarsely ground black pepper

4 salmon steaks (about $1^1/_2$ pounds total)

Serves 4.

Preheat grill to medium-high heat. In a small saucepan, combine brown sugar, bourbon, mustard, soy sauce and pepper. Cook over low heat on the stovetop for 2 minutes, or until sugar has melted, stirring constantly.

Brush salmon with the bourbon sauce and grill 6-8 minutes, or until glazed and fish flakes easily with a fork, turning occasionally. Bring any remaining sauce to a boil and drizzle over salmon before serving.

Artist Jane Wooster Scott has been dazzling locals and visitors for years with her ornate paintings of Sun Valley scenes. From ice skating at the Sun Valley Lodge to skiing Baldy's slopes, Jane's delightful attention to detail makes us want to jump right into the action.

COD SUPREME ALA NORTH

FROM LEIF ODMARK

Serve this recipe with chilled white wine or a Pouilly Fousse.

1$\frac{1}{2}$ pounds cod

1 cup dry wine

$\frac{1}{4}$ cup seasoned breadcrumbs

1 cup lowfat plain yogurt

$\frac{1}{4}$ cup chopped green onion

Paprika

Serves 6.

Place fish in baking dish. Pour wine over cod and marinate in fridge for 15-30 minutes.

Discard wine and pat fish dry with paper towels. Dip both sides in bread-crumbs. Place fish back in baking dish.

Combine yogurt and green onions and spread over fish. Sprinkle with paprika.

Bake in 400°F oven about 15-20 minutes or until fish flakes when tested with fork.

Serve with baked potatoes and steamed carrots.

A resident of the Wood River Valley since the 1940s, Leif was a US Olympic (Oslo, Norway, 1952) coach and a Goodwill Ambassador to the 1972 Sapporo Olympic Games in Japan. Leif founded and owned the Sun Valley Nordic Ski School and Touring Center for 18 years, the first of its kind in the US. Leif remains active in the sports world and holds a course record in the St. George Marathon in the 60-years-and-over age category. He is one of the top Alpine Master Ski Racers in the USA in his age group.

Leif has found Sun Valley to be a wonderful place to live, with its fresh air and good water. And, he declares, "The local people are the best!" In the winter, he spends his time skiing Baldy, "one of the best resorts in the world," and Nordic skiing our long, beautiful groomed trails. In the summer-time, Leif enjoys golfing, mountain biking, hiking, running and fishing.

HONEY-SOY AHI

FROM CHRIS & KATRINA CORD

This is Chris's favorite recipe… and Katrina's, too, since he does all the shopping and cooking!

4 sushi-grade ahi tuna steaks, about 6 ounces each and $1\frac{1}{2}$ inches thick

Marinade

$\frac{1}{4}$ cup soy sauce

2 tablespoons honey

1 tablespoon Asian sesame oil

1 tablespoon grated fresh ginger

$\frac{1}{2}$ teaspoon ground black pepper

In a small bowl, whisk together all marinade ingredients. Place tuna in a large resealable plastic bag and add the marinade. Press the air out of the bag and seal tightly. Turn the bag to distribute the marinade. Place bag with tuna and marinade in a bowl and refrigerate for about 30 minutes.

Remove steaks from the bag and discard marinade. Grill steaks over direct high heat on an open grill just until the surface is well marked and the center of the steaks is red (about 3-4 minutes). Turn once halfway through grilling time. Remove from grill and serve.

Chris and Katrina Cord

Christopher Cord, grandson of the famous 1930s auto manufacturer E.L. Cord, won the 1987 National Driving Championship for Dan Gurney and Toyota; Katrina was chief cook and bottle washer for his 24-man team. Chris is still racing cars, but of the vintage variety, and mainly in California.

The Cords were attracted to this incredible area because of the beauty and the numerous outdoor activities. The warmth of the residents and their commitment to maintaining a high degree of excellence in the community proved to be the "frosting on the cake"! Chris and Katrina, now full-time residents, are very involved in the St. Luke's Hospital Auxiliary and the St. Thomas Church.

CHILEAN SEA BASS AND GINGER

FROM RIDLEY PEARSON

Chilean sea bass

Fresh ginger, chopped or grated

Soy sauce

Marinate the sea bass in the freshly chopped or grated ginger and soy sauce for at least 20 minutes. Cook in the microwave between 2-5 minutes, depending upon the size of the fish. This cooks the inside a bit first. Then broil about 5 minutes per side, again depending upon the thickness of the fish. Simple and delicious.

Whether it's writing frighteningly real suspense fiction, playing bass guitar in a literary all-star garage band, or the inherent joys of new fatherhood, Ridley Pearson has mastered the art of keeping a lot of people up at night. With thirteen highly praised thrillers under his belt best-selling author Pearson has earned a reputation for writing novels that grip the imagination, emphasize forensic detail, and, all too often, imitate life. Nearly all of Pearson's novels have been optioned for film, including *No Witnesses*, which stars Jamie Lee Curtis.

Ridley was raised in Connecticut and now lives in the Northwest with his wife, Marcelle, and daughters, Paige and Storey. He first came to Idaho over 20 years ago to help his brother, Brad, finish a film script, and he never left. He and his family have a home in Hailey where they spend summers and vacations, and when Ridley releases a new novel, he comes to Sun Valley for book signings.

MOM'S FRIDAY-NIGHT TUNA CASSEROLE

FROM DANIELLE KENNEDY

I served up lots of tuna casserole to my eight children. They still consider it comfort food and request it when visiting on those cold winter nights!

4-5 green onions, chopped

4-5 celery stalks, chopped

$^1/_4$ cup butter (half a stick)

Fresh mushrooms, chopped, or 2 cans mushrooms, drained

1 pound elbow macaroni

2 cans tuna in spring water

1 can cream of mushroom soup

1 cup low-fat milk

Cheddar cheese

In a skillet, sauté green onions and celery in butter. Add mushrooms and cook until tender. Stir in cream of mushroom soup and milk and blend well. Bring to a boil for just a second, then simmer for 5 minutes.

Boil elbow macaroni until al dente; drain and set aside.

Drain cans of tuna into a paper towel and set aside.

In a large casserole dish sprayed with Pam, combine the mushroom mixture with drained macaroni and tuna. Sprinkle with a layer of cheddar cheese and cover dish with tin foil. Bake for 35 minutes in a 350°F oven. Remove foil covering and allow cheese to burn slightly, about 5 more minutes. Serve hot!

Local actress, author and motivational speaker Danielle Kennedy has moved both local and national audiences. Since becoming a part of Company of Fools in 1997, her acting credits include Patsy in *Side Man*, Dorothea in *Eleemosynary*, Penny in *You Can't Take It With You*, Giant's wife in *Jack and the Beanstalk*, May in *The Philadelphia Story* and Mom in Bruce Willis's production of *True West*. Danielle has also directed several Company of Fools productions, including *What Happened Was* and *How I Learned to Drive*. She's taught the company's Stages of Wonders and studies acting with Rusty Wilson and Walt Witcover, and her motivational speeches have opened for the likes of Colin Powell.

BASQUE PAELLA

FROM CARRIE CENARRUSA, REPRESENTING IDAHO'S BASQUE COMMUNITY

$1/4$ cup olive oil

2 chorizos, crumbled

1 yellow onion, finely chopped

4 garlic cloves, minced

1 green pepper, finely chopped

$1/2$ cup chopped pimiento

1 large tomato, peeled, seeded and finely diced

2 cups long-grain rice (Uncle Ben's)

$3 1/2$ cups clam juice

1 cup white port

1 pinch saffron

Salt & pepper to taste

10 whole clams in the shell, well scrubbed

12 large shrimp, shelled and deveined

$1/2$ pound crabmeat

$1/2$ pound chicken, cooked and cubed

9-ounce package frozen artichoke hearts

$1/2$ cup peas

Serves 8 – 10.

In a 4-quart saucepan, heat olive oil. Add crumbled chorizo; cook while stirring, about 3 minutes. Add onion, garlic and green pepper. Add pimiento and tomato, sauté gently until most of the liquid has evaporated and onion is tender.

Preheat oven to 350°F. Stir rice, clam juice, port, saffron, salt and pepper into chorizo mixture. Bring to boil. As soon as mixture boils, transfer to a large paella pan or 4-quart casserole dish. Bake covered for 40 minutes. Stir in whole clams, shrimp, crab, chicken, artichoke hearts and peas. Cover and bake for another 10 minutes.

Today, the sheep herding days are pretty much over for the Basques in the American West, but their cooking legacy remains. Basques have created enclaves of their rich culture from California to Idaho: If you have ever attended any of the Basque festivals that occur in the summertime throughout Idaho, you have had a taste. The Wood River Valley has an abundance of Basques, and you can sample their cooking, along with other cultural events, at the local festival held each summer.

Carrie Cenarrusa

SEA BASS MEDITERRANEAN STYLE

FROM CLINT EASTWOOD

This recipe is compliments of The Restaurant at Mission Ranch, proprietors Craig and Cynthia Ling.

4 6-to8-ounce fillets
of sea bass

4 ripe tomatoes

3 teaspoons minced garlic

1½ tablespoons capers

10 Kalamata olives,
coarsely chopped

1 teaspoon fennel seed
or 1 tablespoon Pernod liquor

¼ cup olive oil

1 teaspoon saffron

2 cups rice

½ yellow onion, diced

6 cups water or bouillon

Fresh fennel

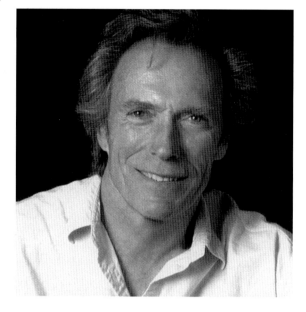

Serves 4.

Mix onion into rice with saffron and water. Cover and bake in medium (350°F) oven until water is almost gone (about 50 minutes).

While rice is baking, start sauce: blanch tomatoes in hot water for 30 seconds, then peel and chop. Put olive oil and garlic into large skillet. When hot, add tomatoes and fennel (or Pernod). Simmer 15 minutes. Add capers and olives and a couple of twists of fresh ground pepper. Remove from heat and keep warm.

Sear fish in hot skillet with a little oil (peanut or vegetable) for 2 minutes on each side, then bake in oven for 6-8 minutes, depending on thickness.

Slice and blanch fresh fennel bulb in salted water for 5 minutes or until tender.

Put rice on one side of each plate, and then spoon sauce over the other side. Place finished sea bass on top of sauce and garnish with fresh fennel.

Clint Eastwood broke hearts in *The Bridges of Madison County*, commanded respect in *Absolute Power*, and baffled us in *Midnight in the Garden of Good and Evil*, and his performances in *True Crime* and *Space Cowboys* led to more box-office hits. His enormous talent has been recognized by the Academy Awards in 1992, when *Unforgiven* was awarded best picture and he was awarded best director for the film; by the Irving G. Thalberg Memorial Award in 1995, one of the most highly regarded awards for accomplishments in film as an actor, director or producer; and in 2000 as an honoree of The Kennedy Center Honors.

Of course, most Wood River Valley locals still revere *Pale Rider* as a favorite, filmed right here in our own backyard, with many residents hired as extras. Clint Eastwood is as much a part of Sun Valley as he is of cowboy and Dirty Harry movies. And if you get up early enough on an epic powder day, you might get a glimpse of Clint as he disappears into the heavenly fluff, always wearing a grin.

SHRIMP & SCALLOPS BAKED WITH FENNEL AND PARMESAN FROM DAVINCI'S

16 shrimp, large, peeled and deveined

16 sea scallops, large

$1/2$ cup olive oil

3 tablespoons Dijon mustard

3 tablespoons garlic, minced

Pepper, freshly ground, to taste

Kosher salt, to taste

1 cup fennel leaves, chopped

1 cup Italian parsley, chopped

1 cup butter, unsalted, softened

1 cup bread crumbs, plain

1 cup parmesan cheese, grated

4 sprigs of fresh fennel, for garnish

In a small bowl, whisk together oil, mustard, garlic, salt and pepper.

Place 4 shrimp and 4 scallops in individual baking dishes and brush with oil mixture.

In a food processor combine fennel, parsley, and butter, and place a teaspoon of butter mixture on each shrimp.

Mix together in a small bowl bread crumbs and parmesan cheese and top each baking dish with $1/2$ cup of the bread crumb mixture.

Bake for 10-15 minutes in a 375°F oven or until seafood is cooked through. Garnish with a sprig of fresh fennel.

Larry and Jennifer Schwartz met while attending Cornell University and moved to the Wood River Valley after graduation. They worked in various restaurants in town and in Washington state before starting daVinci's in Hailey in 1996, and in Eagle, Idaho in 1998. Both daVinci's offer classical and enticing Italian fare, and keep Larry and Jennifer busy. But they still find time to enjoy all the wonderful things the Wood River Valley has to offer.

BAJA SHRIMP

FROM BING COPELAND

12 jumbo shrimp, shelled,
butterflied and deveined

4 cloves fresh garlic, finely chopped

2 tablespoons chopped cilantro

$1/4$ cup butter

Serves 4.

Melt butter in a skillet. Add garlic and sauté until garlic starts to brown. Add shrimp and cook until shrimp turns opaque, then sprinkle cilantro over shrimp and leave on the stove another 30 seconds or so.

Place shrimp on plates and serve with steamed rice and sliced melon. Pour remaining butter, garlic & cilantro from skillet over shrimp and rice.

Bing Copeland and his friend, Greg Noll, began surfing at the Manhattan Beach pier in 1949 at the tender age of 13. The two surfing gremmies regularly hung around Velzy's first shop until 1955, when Bing moved to Hawaii to surf. In 1958, Bing and Rick Stoner sailed to Tahiti and eventually to New Zealand, where they introduced modern surfing to the Kiwis.

Bing opened up his first surf shop in the fall of 1959 and became one of the major surfboard manufacturers of the '60s and early '70s. Bing and his family currently live in the mountains of Idaho and spend their winters surfing and sailing the warm waters of southern Baja.

Scrumptious Shrimp Scampi

FROM JOHN & MAGGI KELLY

This is absolutely delicious and combines two important ingredients in our Sun Valley lifestyle: style and ease. And if you think that scampi is just scampi, we really recommend this new version. The sauce combines wine, garlic, lemon, and butter with browned pan drippings, so it must be served with a wonderful, crusty French bread for dipping. Add salad and steamed asparagus and you have a not-to-be-forgotten dinner. For variation, serve the scampi over risotto or pasta.

2 pounds large shrimp, peeled, deveined, butterflied (tails on to minimize curling)

1 cup flour

1 cup olive oil

1½ cups dry white wine

1 tablespoon Worcestershire sauce

5 cloves garlic, minced

5 tablespoons lemon juice, fresh

½ cup chicken stock (fresh is always best, but you can use canned)

¼ pound butter, cut into pieces

Salt & freshly ground black pepper to taste

2 tablespoons fresh parsley, minced

Serves 6.

Dredge shrimp in flour. Heat olive oil in large skillet over medium-high heat. Working in batches, sauté shrimp until just golden (they don't need to be fully cooked at this point). Transfer to a plate lined with paper towels to drain off oil, and continue until all shrimp are cooked. NOTE: As shrimp are cooking, the flour in the skillet should become a golden brown. Do not let it burn, as it is the basis for the sauce.

Drain excess oil from pan, leaving flour in the bottom. Stir in wine, Worcestershire, garlic, lemon juice, and chicken stock. Cook over medium-high heat until reduced by a third to one-half, depending on the consistency you desire. Whisk in butter, salt and pepper. Lower heat and add shrimp to reheat (ensuring that they are fully cooked but not overdone). Coat well with the sauce and sprinkle with parsley. Serve immediately, and don't forget the bread!

John F. Kelly is the Chairman & CEO of Alaska Airlines and Chairman of Sun Valley's own Horizon Air. Competing with his lifelong love of the airline business is his love of the beautiful Sun Valley area. He and his wife, Maggi, together with their daughter, Shannon, enjoy their frequent stays in their home in Warm Springs.

Theirs is a common story. They came here to ski and fell in love with this glorious place, with its unpretentious, casual lifestyle — where wonderful people are connected through common interests of all things outdoors . . . and where dogs rule.

MATS'S PEEL & EAT SHRIMP WITH BROWN RICE

FROM MATS WILANDER

Shrimp:

2 tablespoons butter

2 tablespoons olive oil

2 pounds jumbo shrimp, cleaned and deveined with shells on

3 cloves fresh garlic, crushed

1 small yellow onion, chopped

$1/2$ cup white wine

2 tablespoons fresh lemon juice

4-5 thin slices lemon
(save the rest for garnish)

3 tablespoons Italian flat parsley, chopped

Salt & pepper to taste

Brown Rice:

2 cups brown Basmati rice, rinsed and drained

$1/2$ small onion, diced

4 cups vegetable broth

1 tablespoon butter

Shrimp: Heat oil and butter in a large skillet. Add onions, garlic and lemon slices. Sauté until onions are translucent. Add shrimp and sauté on one side (2-3 minutes) until turning pink. Turn shrimp over, add wine, lemon juice, salt and pepper. When shrimp is nearly done, add Italian parsley. Toss and serve with brown rice.

Brown Rice: Sauté onion in butter until soft. Add rice and sauté rice and onion for 2 minutes. Slowly add hot broth. Bring to a boil, reduce heat and cover. Simmer for 50 minutes, or until done. Let stand for 10 minutes. Fluff with a fork and serve.

At the tender age of 17, tennis pro Mats Wilander won the 1982 French Open, the first of seven career Grand Slam titles. In all, he won three French Opens, three Australian Opens and one U.S. Open. In 1988, he won three Grand Slams and became the seventh player to reach No. 1 in the history of the ATP Tour Rankings, making him the 1988 ATP Player of the Year. And Swedish-born Wilander came of age on the Senior Circuit in 1999, winning three titles on three different continents — in Europe, America and Asia.

Perhaps it's his passion for art and music that keeps him going. Or his enjoyment of golf . . . or his love for his family—wife, Sonya, and children Emma, Karl and Oskar. Or maybe, just maybe, it's the time he takes for a little R & R in Sun Valley, where he and his family moved to "get away." Mats appreciates the peace and quiet, and likes to downhill and cross-country ski.

COQUILLE ST. JACQUES

FROM JOE FOS

This recipe is my wife Patricia's own creation, and I encourage everyone to experience it. Rich-tasting and high in protein, it rivals any you have tasted! All you need to round out this meal is some dry white wine, warm crusty bread and a hearty green leafy salad. Poached Pears for dessert go well with this delicate seafood dish. When all the ingredients are prepared and assembled, it takes approximately 20 minutes to put dinner on the table. Everything in this meal can be prepared ahead of time so a host and hostess can enjoy their company before, during and after dinner.

1 coarsely sliced shallot

$1/2$ pound scallops

$1/4$ pound crabmeat

$1/4$ pound clean boiled shrimp

$3/4$ cup dry white wine
Pinot Grigio

$1/2$ cup sliced fresh mushrooms

1 cup Hollandaise Sauce
(recipe below)

$1/2$ pound butter

2 cups prepared
mashed potatoes

Serves 4.

Sauté shallot in butter just until tender, but do not brown. Strain shallot from butter and discard. Add mushrooms and sauté until tender. Add wine and simmer. Add all seafood and simmer 10 minutes, covered. Remove mixture from heat.

Arrange scallop shells (or other decorative, oven-proof dishes) onto crumpled foil on a sturdy baking sheet and spray with Pam (this is important!). Preheat oven to 425°F.

Add half the Hollandaise Sauce to mixture and blend completely. Add a heaping tablespoon of mashed potatoes to mixture and blend well to thicken sauce. Spoon enough mixture into each shell so it's $1/2$ inch from the top. Using a pastry sieve, ring the edge of each shell with mashed potatoes, or spoon them on carefully, being careful not to mix them together. Sprinkle potatoes with finely rubbed parsley flecks (not flakes!) and a light sprinkle of paprika, for color. Spoon a heaping tablespoon of Hollandaise in the middle of each shell mixture; do not mix in. Pop into the oven for 10 minutes and serve immediately.

Hollandaise Sauce:
$1/2$ cup (1 stick) melted butter

Into blender put:
3 egg yolks
1 tablespoon lemon juice
$1/4$ teaspoon salt
Pinch of cayenne

Blend on LOW speed. Immediately pour in hot butter in a steady stream. DO NOT STOP pouring until all the butter is added and then immediately turn off blender. Pour sauce into a bowl and let sit at room temperature until needed.

Pianist Joe Fos began his legendary career at the age of 14 when he won a competition over 150 other youths by performing "Hungarian Rhapsody No. 2" and subsequently appeared in concert with Liberace. Joe received a scholarship to the Julliard School of Music and has been Sun Valley's resident pianist since 1979.

Joe has played in Los Angeles, where Robert Goulet nicknamed him "14 fingers Fos," and appeared on television with the Walt Disney Fantasy on Ice Christmas special. He is the host of the annual Sun Valley Swing 'n' Dixie Jazz Jamboree music festival and a special guest soloist for the Sun Valley Symphony. The "Joe Fos Trio" performs nightly in the Duchin Room of the Sun Valley Lodge, constantly evoking the ambience and old-world elegance of its original grand era through the music he plays. Even more extraordinary, Joe's unparalleled performances are all from his remarkable memory!